MARRIAGE IN INTERESTING TIMES

A PARTICIPATORY STUDY GUIDE

ROBERT D. CORNWALL

Energion Publications
Gonzalez, FL
2016

Cover Image: Adobe Stock, 56532756
Cover Design: Henry E. Neufeld

ISBN10: 1-63199-227-9
ISBN13: 978-1-63199-227-8
Library of Congress Control Number: 2016938021

Energion Publications
P. O. Box 841
Gonzalez, Fl 32560

energion.com
pubs@energion.com

The meaning of marriage is a multi-layered discussion in the early twenty-first century. What is marriage from biblical and theological perspectives? Who can marry? What are characteristics of a good committed relationship? How can people live with one another so as to foster the most important qualities of marriage? Dr. Robert Cornwall, a recognized and insightful Christian interpreter of our times, takes up these and other questions in this study guide which can be used by individuals reading alone and by groups. He considers key biblical texts and their implications for thinking about marriage today, calling attention to similarities as well as differences. At the same time, Cornwall goes beyond Bible study to theological reflection and to practical considerations. I am impressed by the breadth of his research and by the clarity with which he writes. Each chapter includes questions for personal reflection or group discussion, a call to prayer, and a practical call to action—something we can do in our everyday lives to enhance our understanding of marriage and our marriage practices.

Ronald J. Allen, Ph.D.
Professor of Gospels, Letters and Preaching
Christian Theological Seminary

Interesting times indeed. This moment in our history begs the Body of Christ to embrace as never before human suffering in all its dizzying complexity. Nowhere is that need more central than for an understanding of marriage as it engages the biblical story, while considering its meaning in our time. Here comes Dr. Robert Cornwall to invite a lively, creative, and grace-filled conversation — to reason together in love. His is an invitation to a conversation that replaces exclusion, pat answers, and glib God-talk with wisdom, compassion, and grace. Come join the conversation!

Luann Adams, LMFT, RN
Individual, Marriage, & Family Therapist
Registered Nurse, author & speaker

How many times have you been told what the Bible says about marriage? Isn't it time you took a look for yourself? *Marriage in Interesting Times* by Robert Cornwall is just the place to start. Rev.

Cornwall covers all the bases related to marriage and family: How does marriage fit into our lives and our culture? What is marriage for? And singleness? What about marriage and sex and children? And divorce? Have you thought about marriage and eternity? Rev. Cornwall provides a thoughtful and thought provoking essay on each of the ten scriptures he has selected for this study guide. And perhaps more important, this guide provides provocative questions for reflection on each scripture alongside a call to action on each scripture, encouraging us to learn more and live out the biblical message. This book is an excellent resource for personal and group reflection on the Bible's message on marriage in our interesting times.

Rev. Mark C. Johnston, Ph.D., Executive Director
Open and Affirming Ministry Program
Gay Lesbian and Affirming Disciples Alliance

All too often, biblical texts about marriage are flattened into soundbites, divorced from historical context and emptied of wisdom. In *Marriage in Interesting Times*, Bob Cornwall masterfully guides readers through the nuance and complexity of biblical teachings about marriage, and invites us to explore their meaning in light of our contemporary context. The times are very interesting, indeed — and so is this book!

Rev. Katherine Willis Pershey
Associate Minister, First Congregational Church of Western Springs
Author of *Any Day a Beautiful Change: A Story of Faith and Family*

TABLE OF CONTENTS

Acknowledgements v

The Participatory Study Series vi

Using this Book vii

1   Biblical Marriage and Cultural Realities 1
     – Genesis 29:15-30

2   Fit Companions 11
     – Genesis 2:18-24

3   Fit Companions? What If I'm Single? 19
     – 1 Corinthians 7:1-7, 32-35

4   How to Find a Mate (or Not)? 29
     – Hosea 1:2-9

5   It's a Covenant not a Contract! 35
     – Ruth 1

6   Marriage and Sex Go Together 43
     – Song of Songs 7; 8

7   Marriage: A Partnership of Equals 55
     – 1 Corinthians 7:1-7

8   Fruitful and Multiplying
     – Family and Expanding the Community 65
       – Genesis 1:26-31

9   When Things Don't Work – The Reality of Divorce 75
     – Mark 10:1-12

10   Beyond Marriage and Family 83
     – Luke 20:27-40

     Bibliography 91

ACKNOWLEDGMENTS

Every book is the product of numerous conversations. This book is no different. It emerged out of conversations within the congregation I serve as pastor (Central Woodward Christian Church of Troy, Michigan), but also from my own experience in marriage. For thirty plus years I've been married to Cheryl. In poverty and prosperity, in good times and not so good times, we have remained committed to each other and to our marriage. Therefore, this study guide is dedicated to Cheryl, even as we continue the journey together.

Over the last several years I have been blessed to be part of the Energion family. My thanks to Henry and Jody Neufeld, my publishers. Henry had encouraged me to write this book and waited patiently for it to come to fruition. I appreciate his willingness to take this on, and provide editorial oversight and encouragement along the way.

I have benefited from the encouragement and words of wisdom from several who have read the manuscript in all or part. Therefore, my gratitude is extended to Steve Kindle, Alexandra McCauslin, Robert LaRochelle, and Chris Eyre. Yes, Cheryl read parts of the book as well. They are not responsible for the book or its contents, but they have all provided me with needed counsel along the way.

My hope and prayer is that the book will prove helpful to the church, to those considering marriage, and those living out the covenant that is marriage. May we all remember that ultimately we belong to the same family, for we are all sisters and brothers of Jesus. May that relationship with God in partnership with Jesus through the auspices of the Holy Spirit bless us all.

Epiphany 2016

The Participatory Study Series

The Participatory Study Series from Energion Publications is designed around the motto "scholarship in service." Each guide is written by someone with a strong background in the topic studied and designed for use by lay people in Sunday School classes and small groups, as well as for individual study.

These guides are not all easy reading. Some of the topics covered require serious effort on the part of the student. But the guides do provide all the resources necessary for a fruitful study.

The section "Using this Book" is designed for the series but adapted to the particular study guide. Each author is free to emphasize different resources in the study, and to follow his or her own plan in presenting the material.

It is our prayer at Energion Publications that each study guide will lead you to a deeper understanding of your Christian faith.

— Henry Neufeld, General Editor

Using the Book

This study guide is designed to be used by small groups, whether a Bible study group, a Sunday School Class, or perhaps a marriage prep class. The commentary has been provided to stimulate conversation about an important aspect of human life—marriage. Whether or not one is married or considering the prospect of being married, individuals also should find the book stimulating, helping them process questions raised by their encounters with the Bible and their own experience of life in the twenty-first century.

At a time when the definition of marriage is evolving, people of faith are seeking to understand the relationship of their faith to these changing dynamics. Many who defend what they call traditional marriage—by which they mean the marriage of "one man to one woman"—look to the Bible for support (along with appeals to nature). Others in our society have called for expanding the definition to include same-sex couples. Many of those on this side of the issue seek to be faithful to Scripture and the tenets of their faith. The question of who should be allowed to be married is being raised by the broader culture in the West (Europe and North America especially). Most polls show that a firm majority of Americans support marriage equality—that is extending the right to marry to same-sex couples on the same basis as opposite sex couples. Then, on June 26, 2015, the United States Supreme Court ruled that same-sex couples had the same right to be married as heterosexual couples. While the extension of the right to marry to same-sex couples does not require faith communities to follow suit, it does at the very least require them to address this change of legal status. With this evolving definition of marriage emerging in our culture, and growing numbers of Christians embracing the change, an appropriate question of the day concerns whether the

Bible has something pertinent to say to this evolving understanding of marriage.

My goal in writing this book is to start a conversation about marriage in all its complexity that engages the biblical story. In the course of using this study guide, whether one is using it for personal study or in a group, readers will be introduced to a series of biblical texts from both Testaments. The discussion questions and experiences are meant to invite participants to engage in a conversation with these ancient sacred texts that will help us make sense of what marriage means in the twenty-first century.

In writing this study guide, I must state up front that I am not an expert on the dynamics of marriage and family. I'm not a therapist nor do I have degrees in marriage and family studies. What I am is a pastor, a theologian, and Bible teacher. To say that I am a teacher of the Bible is not to say that I am a professional biblical scholar—my advanced training is in historical theology not biblical studies. Therefore, my commentary on the biblical passages relies on the expertise of others who are professional biblical scholars. Besides being a pastor, theologian, and Bible teacher, I can speak to some degree about marriage from my own experience, having been married to one woman for more than thirty years.

I titled the study guide "Marriage in Interesting Times," because we are living at a time when there are profound changes in the way marriage is understood. Not that long ago, it was assumed by many in American society that traditional marriage not only involved a man and a woman, but the man was the head of the household and the woman was a homemaker. The man earned the money, and the woman cared for the children and kept the house in order. Then came the idea that husband and wife were equal partners in the marriage. In most cases both partners worked outside the home, and they shared more equally the duties of the home. Today, the definition of marriage has evolved one more time to include same-sex couples. As Supreme Court Justice Anthony Kennedy put it in the concluding paragraph of his majority opinion in *Obergefell v. Hodges* that overturned bans on same-sex marriage across the country:

> No union is more profound than marriage, for it embodies the highest ideals of love, fidelity, devotion, sacrifice, and family. In forming a marital union, two people become something greater than once they were. As some of the petitioners in these cases demonstrate, marriage embodies a love that may endure even past death. It would misunderstand these men and women to say they disrespect the idea of marriage. Their plea is that they do respect it, respect it so deeply that they seek to find its fulfillment for themselves. Their hope is not to be condemned to live in loneliness, excluded from one of civilization's oldest institutions. They ask for equal dignity in the eyes of the law. The Constitution grants them that right.

So, when we talk about marriage in the twenty-first century, at least in the United States, and a number of other nations around the globe, we must remember that the legal definition, if not the religious one, includes both gay and straight couples. Yes, these are interesting times.

Although this is not a book about marriage equality or same-sex marriage, I need to state up front that I am a supporter of marriage equality. For a variety of reasons, I have come to believe that God blesses such unions. One of the reasons why I decided to write this study guide is that I discovered that the sticking point in the full inclusion of Lesbian, Gay, Bisexual, Transgender persons (LGBT) in church (as well as in society as a whole) was the definition of marriage. I found it interesting that many opponents of gay marriage actually support civil unions, believing that all the legal benefits linked to marriage could be made available to same-gender couples, even as the word marriage (holy matrimony) would be reserved for heterosexual couples. The problem is that at least in the United States, civil union doesn't have the same status as marriage. When it comes to the church, especially in churches that seek to be welcoming and inclusive, it strikes many that reserving the word marriage and access to a church wedding makes same-sex couples second class citizens in the church. Now that the government has extended the legal/civil right to marriage to same-sex couples, the word marriage has taken on a new dimension in our society. So in writing this study, I have tried to be sensitive to this evolving definition. The biblical texts that we'll be looking at assume that the partners in a sanctioned relationship will be heterosexuals. While that is true, that doesn't mean that what we read there cannot apply equally to both gay and straight couples.

Having admitted my presuppositions, I also need to note that the study guide is first and foremost focused on marriage, not on the gender of the couples involved. This isn't intended to be read as a definitive statement on marriage either. My hope is that by exploring these texts readers will have the opportunity to consider the wisdom present in the biblical story, even as they wrestle with the evolving nature of our contemporary definitions of marriage. My hope is that in the end, the reader will recognize in the biblical story a witness to the profundity of the marriage covenant. In other words, even if the definition of marriage is evolving, its importance in our society need not be diminished.

Moving on the structure of the study guide: in each chapter, I will provide an overview of the topic and introduce the texts and their contexts. We will consider a number of texts, but will not be addressing all of the possible texts that relate to marriage. Each chapter focuses on a different topic relating to marriage—including divorce and singleness. The study guide provides questions and activities that can help guide the conversation. There are several things you can do to make this study more profitable.

(1) Where **resources** are suggested, divide them between members of the class and consult them during your study time. Students can bring what they have learned to the study. This is also a good time to help your church improve its library. Suggest some of the resources for your library shelves. While this is a topical study, we will be reading the Bible throughout the

study, so bring a Bible, preferably a modern translation. If you are looking for a Bible, I would suggest either the New Revised Standard Version or the Common English Bible. You also might want to consult *The Message*, which is a free translation or paraphrase.

(2) **Share.** The Participatory Study Guides to Bible books pioneered sharing as an integral part of your study, but it will work just as well when you are studying a topic. Sharing does not mean harassing other people with your viewpoint. It's a matter of listening and being accountable in your community. If you come to a conclusion, listen to others who can comment on it and possibly point our reasons that you may be wrong, or ideas that may not have occurred to you.

As a topical study guide this book is intended to be practical in its application. Be sure to think of living the word as you learn it!

CHAPTER 1

BIBLICAL MARRIAGE AND CULTURAL REALITIES

Genesis 29:15-30

We live in interesting times. Not only are women and men delaying marriage and child-bearing, the definition of what constitutes marriage is seemingly being redefined. Court after court across the nation ruled that laws banning same-gender marriages were unconstitutional under the Fourteenth Amendment's "Equal Protection" clause, the United States Supreme Court finally ruled in a 5-4 decision that the states could not deny same-sex couples the right to be married. The changes have been coming fast and furious. For some in American society, the very foundations of our culture seem to be under attack. Traditional definitions of marriage that assume that suitable partners involve one man marrying one woman have been challenged and found wanting by many in society, including growing numbers of people within the Christian community. In the eyes of many, marriage is a divinely established partnership that is designed to provide the proper nesting place for children to be born and mature. This child-centered vision has been found wanting by many, and new understandings have begun emerge. Even if there have always been alternative visions of the family, for some in our society it is difficult to watch long-held traditions seem to disappear.

From the beginning of time people have gotten divorces and even remarried, though these have not always been sanctioned by religious bodies. People have also gotten married without any intention of having children, or have stayed married even though having children isn't possible. There is also a newer phenomenon in which seniors are living together without the benefit of marriage lest they lose their full Social Security benefits. It was into this mix that the call for marriage equality entered. As the stigma of being gay lessened in recent years, same-gender couples have pushed for the opportunity to be married in the eyes of the state (and God/church) in the same way that has been accorded heterosexual couples. In part this is due to the fact that the state grants certain rights and privileges to traditional male-female couples that are not granted to same-gender couples, even if states have offered civil unions as an alternative.

There are in essence two forums for the discussion, which in the United States seem to be intertwined. There is "legal" marriage, which in essence is a contract entered into by two parties and affirmed by the state. There is also religiously sanctioned marriage, which as we will see is defined in covenant terms and is in essence affirmed by God. In many cases clergy represent both church and state as they preside over ceremonies uniting couples in marriage. While there are debates raging about whether clergy should act as agents of the state, for much of American history they have fulfilled both roles.

For Christians there are theological issues that need to be addressed when it comes to marriage and family. At the center of the theological discussion stands the Bible. Many opponents of same-gender marriage believe that the change in the law undermines what they believe to be "biblical marriage." Since we often hear people talk about the "biblical definition of marriage," perhaps it would be good to explore what marriage looks like in the Bible and how the Bible speaks to our own situation today. That will be the focus of this study guide.

There is an assumption on the part of many that what we know to be traditional marriage is the same thing as biblical marriage. We often hear people say that same-sex marriage would undermine two thousand years and more of biblical teaching, but is this true? The real question is whether there is such a thing as a "biblical" definition of marriage? Or is marriage something that is culturally defined and evolves over time?

Before we can think about how marriage is understood in the Bible, we might want to consider the role that marriage plays in our own society. In his manifesto on marriage, practical theologian Tony Jones reminds us that there are in fact two marriages in America—a legal one and a sacred one. "Legal marriage" is state-sanctioned. There are laws that stipulate who can and who cannot be legally married. There are age limits. They speak to whether or not persons of the same family can be married—incest is forbidden. And until recently legal marriage has been limited to male/female partnerships. Tony notes that while there are 515 benefits afforded to married couples that are not given to non-married couples, therefore "legal marriage has nothing to do with sexual intimacy."[1] In other words, the government isn't really interested in what you do in the bedroom, as long as you fit the proper categories stipulated by the laws of the states. Sacred marriage, on the other hand, has nothing to with what the state deems necessary or proper. Rather, it is focused on what God deems to be appropriate. Since the Bible and Christian tradition do talk about sex, God would seem to be interested in what goes on between two people in the bedroom and outside it. As Tony reminds us, this is where we get into interpretive debates.

While the state has empowered clergy to represent it in matters of marriage—at least in signing off on the marriage certificate—the state doesn't really give the church or clergy much of a legal role once the papers are filed. If a marriage ends, the government doesn't invite clergy to participate in the process of dissolution (in the Roman Catholic Church there is a process of annulment, but it is different from divorce).

So, what role should the church and its clergy play in our current cultural realities? There are, for instance, clergy who feel it is appropriate to bless same-sex relationships, considering them sacred in the eyes of God. Others do not. Should the state determine, which kind of relationships are appropriate (as long as they

---

1   Tony Jones, *There are Two Marriages: A Manifesto on Marriage,* (Minneapolis: Jopa Productions, 2011, loc. 49).

are consenting adults and do not pose a danger to society)? It's not only an issue for same-sex couples. As I noted, many older couples choose to live together without benefit of marriage, because if they are legally wed their Social Security benefits will be diminished. Should the church bless their relationships, even if this means helping them evade the law? These kinds of issues have helped trigger the conversation about whether it would be a good thing for the church to sever its relationship with the state when it comes to participating in the legal side of the marriage contract made between two consenting adults.

There are, it would seem, important legal questions that we would be wise to consider. But, this is not a study guide focused on what the government deems appropriate. Rather we are embarking on a conversation that asks the question—what does the Bible have to say to us about marriage, sex, divorce, singleness, and the way in which the church and the Christian community are involved in this conversation?

A quick read through the Hebrew Bible (Old Testament) will reveal that many, at least among the elite, in ancient Israel, practiced polygamy. Abraham had at least two wives (more likely four); David had several of his own; while Solomon had a harem numbering in the hundreds if not thousands of wives and concubines. Is this biblical marriage?

It would seem that by the first century, if not earlier, polygamy had given way to monogamy. But polygamy is clearly a form of marriage present in the biblical story, and at no point is it specifically prohibited. Monogamy was also the assumed form of marriage within Greco-Roman culture, though allowance was often made for men to be sexually active outside of marriage (men were understood to be bi-sexual and had needs that needed to be accommodated, though the same could not be said for women).[2] Thus, even if marriage was monogamous in the culture in which Christianity was planted, it wasn't necessarily sexually monogamous.

---

2   Margaret A. Farley, *A Framework for Christian Social Ethics*, (New York: Continuum Books, 2006), p. 28.

As we read the biblical story, it's not just a matter of polygamy versus monogamy. There is also the issue of the strong patriarchalism present in this story. While the Bible does include in the story a number of strong women, by and large authority is given to men. First fathers—then husbands are in charge. Wives were usually considered to be property to be dealt with as fathers and husbands deem appropriate. They might be cherished perhaps, but not always. The first priority, it would seem, is to provide children. Sarah and Hannah struggled with their barrenness, and found blessing in giving birth to a child. Of course, there are passages, such as Song of Songs that speak of a deep tenderness between couples, there is also the story of Hosea who marries not for love but because his marriage to a prostitute served as a prophetic symbol.

It is clear that when it comes to marriage and family, the biblical story offers us a complex picture. If this is true, then what can we learn from this ancient sacred text that could speak to our day? Must we, to be faithful to our roots, restore biblical patterns? Or can we look to these stories and theological statements as a starting point for a conversation that can strengthen covenant relationships and enable those, who for whatever reason, are not in such a relationship to find a sense of fulfillment and purpose?

Why this study guide? As a pastor of a congregation that was wrestling with the question of gay marriage or marriage equality, I came to the conclusion that for the conversation to move forward we needed to have a conversation about what the Bible says about the "sacred" form of marriage. While this is not a book on gay marriage or marriage equality, it is my belief that we need to have a larger conversation about marriage and the Bible if we're going to resolve the question of marriage equality. Therefore, it is my assumption that the texts under consideration can apply equally to heterosexual and same-sex marriages. Consider a passage such as Genesis 2, where God looks at the creation, and discerns that the man God had created and placed in the garden is lonely. When God sees this, God creates a companion fit for the man. What is the message of that passage? Is it the story of companionship or heterosexual marriage? While procreation might be part of the story, is it the entire focus of a marriage relationship?

One could look at a passage like 1 Corinthians 7, where Paul seems to prefer the single life to the married state. But he also writes that if one doesn't have the gift of celibacy, then one should get married rather than burn with lust. Surely that is not a rousing endorsement of marriage! Or is it, from Paul's perspective, a realistic one. Human beings do have a sexual drive and in Paul's mind, it is best for that drive to be contained within the marriage relationship. That, of course, raises the question of what happens if one is attracted not to a person of the opposite gender, but of one's own gender. Should there be a provision for such an attraction within our theology of marriage?

As we begin this journey, I think the story of Jacob and his marriages might be instructive. In this story, Isaac and Rebecca decide that it would be better if Jacob found a wife among their own clan, rather than from within the Canaanite community (Genesis 28:1-5). As the story goes, Jacob meets Rachel, the daughter of Laban, the brother of Rebecca. Apparently it's okay to marry first cousins in "biblical times."[3] He falls in love and seeks Rachel's hand in marriage. Laban agrees to the transaction (yes this was a transaction), though Jacob is going to have to work for seven years before he can marry his beloved. Now, that seems rather long, doesn't it? Would you wait seven years to get married?

Jacob works the seven years, and then on the wedding day, Laban sends in his daughter to Jacob's tent. The "happy couple" consummates the marriage. Then the next morning, to his surprise, Jacob wakes up and finds that the woman with whom he has shared a bed isn't his beloved Rachel, but is instead her older sister—Leah. Jacob is furious. He's been tricked, which is a reversal of fortune since it's usually Jacob who is the trickster, and he won't stand for being taken advantage of.

---

3   I might add that Jacob's grandparents, Abraham and Sarah, were not only married, but they were siblings (it appears that they had different mothers, but the same father). See Genesis 20:1-18.

What is interesting about this story is Laban's response to Jacob. Laban simply says to his nephew and now son-in-law: This is not done in our country—giving the younger before the first-born. Now Jacob will eventually receive Rachel as his wife, but Rachel will be his second wife. He might love her more than he loves Leah, which is the cause of tension going forward, but the point that Laban makes is that community standards will prevail. These might not be Jacob's standards, but they are Laban's, and he's going to enforce them.

What is the implication of this story for us? Obviously, we will likely find abhorrent the idea that one must purchase a spouse, even if that means working for seven years. We might want to side with Leah, who gets married, but remains unloved. She has lovely eyes, we're told, but Rachel has the good figure. Could it be that the way we understand marriage evolves over time?

Definitions differ from one community to another. In many cultures, polygamy is still acceptable. In Africa the practice of polygamy has been a major concern for churches. If the churches demand that converts become monogamous, then what happens to those women who are numbered among the additional wives? Will they be abandoned? Is this just? Is it necessary, at least in the near term?

In Laban's mind—in his community—you won't find younger daughters getting married before the older one. It's simply not done.

In the United States, which is where I live, it wasn't that long ago that many states had on their books laws that prohibited inter-racial marriage. Those laws have long been repealed and for the most part society has welcomed inter-racial marriage. In the early twenty-first century it was suggested that the same obstacles were being put in the way of gay and lesbian couples seeking to be married, which led to the Supreme Court decision extending marriage to same-sex couples. The response of some in our society is a bit like that of Laban—we just don't do that kind of thing in our community. But, while Jacob acquiesced to Laban's rules, apparently this wasn't the rule in his own community. At least he wasn't aware of the tradition of Laban's country.

There is much in this story about deception—Jacob was a deceiver, got deceived, and will deceive again. There are also the cultural dynamics present. Even though it does appear that Jacob and Rachel loved each other, Laban wasn't as concerned about their affection for each other as he was in making sure the oldest daughter didn't get pushed aside. I'm not sure that Laban was concerned about Leah's feelings either. I think he was more concerned about making sure he got his money's worth out of his investment in his older daughter. If it appeared that Leah wasn't marriage material, he would lose his investment. In the end Jacob agrees to accept Leah, while he worked off the debt incurred if he was going to receive Rachel's hand. Unfortunately for Leah, there doesn't seem to be much love in his heart for her.

What is interesting is that as the story continues, God sees Leah's plight and blesses her with children, even as Rachel finds it difficult to have children. Blessings come in different ways in the biblical story.

The question that this story poses for us is how we should read these stories and the way in which they speak to marriage customs. How do we separate out what was cultural and what is relevant going forward into the present?

A CALL TO REFLECTION AND CONVERSATION

1. What is the role of marriage in American life?
2. How has marriage and family life changed over the past several decades?
3. How does the Supreme Court ruling affect your view of marriage and that of the church?
4. Do you feel like these changes have been good or not? Why or why not?
5. What do you make of the story of Jacob, his two wives, and his father-in-law?

6. Is there a biblical definition of marriage? If so, what do you think it is?

A Call to Action

If you have internet access, go to the local county clerk's site, and look up the state marriage regulations. Find out who can get married and who is not qualified. Then compare what you find there with another state, preferably one from another part of the country. Reflect on the similarities and differences.

A Call to Prayer

O perfect Love, all human thought transcending, lowly we kneel in prayer before thy throne, that theirs may be the love which knows no ending, whom thou forevermore dost join in one.

Dorothy Frances Blomfield Gurney

CHAPTER 2

FIT COMPANIONS

Genesis 2:18-25

W hy do people get married? Is it because we have a biological need to procreate? You could probably make a scientific case that humans, like most species, have a biological instinct to be fruitful and multiply. But, you don't have to get married for that to occur. While some species do seem to mate for life, they appear to do so without benefit of clergy. So, why do people join together in the institution of marriage? Why go to all the trouble of having a sacred ceremony when legally all that is required is a signed wedding license? Is it simply because children are the expected outcome of the relationship, whose interests need to be protected by a legal mechanism? And, if having children is the primary reason why people get married, then why do people get married who are past child-bearing years or who have no intention of having children?

The creation stories found in Genesis 1 and 2 offer us a primal vision of human community. Both of the creation stories suggest that humans were created to live in community, and one form that community takes is something that looks like marriage. In Genesis 1, the author of this first creation story declares that humankind was created in the image of God as male and female. God then gave to humankind (as male and female) dominion or stewardship over creation. God blessed them and told the first couple to "be fruitful and multiply, and fill the earth and subdue it." While this first creation story does suggest that procreation is part of the human equation, is this the sole purpose for marriage? It is important to remember that the culture in which this story emerged was patriarchal in nature, and yet this story treats the two original humans as equals. Both men and women are created in God's image, and therefore as God's image bearers they stand before God as equals.

Genesis 2 offers us a different creation story that is earthier than the first. God takes a more hands-on approach to creation. If we are to find a word about marriage here, it is going to be less abstract than the first. In this story God creates a man—Adam—from the dust of the ground, and then God breathes life into the man. As you can see; in this story God ends up with dirty hands. When God sets the man in the garden, the man is given access to all the trees in the garden as a food source, except the tree of knowledge of good and evil, which is off-limits to him.

After a bit of time goes by, God, who seems to have been enjoying a conversation with the man, notices that "it is not good that the man should be alone." Indeed, God discerns that the man needs a partner who is fit to him, and God is not that partner.

This is an important recognition on God's part, because for the first time in the creation story, God discovers that something isn't right. After every previous act of creation, God has pronounced it to be good. That includes the creation of the man. This time, God doesn't pronounce things to be good. Something is missing, because it appears to God that being alone is not good for the man. Therefore, God sets out to rectify the situation.

Wanting to make sure that everything is good, God goes back to the drawing board. The first attempt to solve this problem entailed creating non-human creatures. The man gives a name to each creature that God presents to him, but none of these creatures—living on land or in the air—is that fit companion for the man. The man remains alone and incomplete.

Since nothing that God has presented to the man will suffice, God must start fresh. This time God puts the man into a deep sleep, takes a rib, and fashions the rib into a new being—the woman. When God presents the woman to the man, the man shouts with joy:

"This at last is bone of my bones and flesh of my flesh;
this one shall be called Woman (*ishshah*), for out of Man (*ish*)
this one was taken."

The passage continues in a way that is often repeated at weddings— "therefore a man leaves his father and his mother and clings to his wife, and they become one flesh" (Genesis 2:24).

Nothing is said here about reproduction or about being fruitful and multiplying. In fact, nothing is said about sex at all. The man simple recognizes the woman will be a fit companion since she shares the same substance with the man. Being of the same substance (same species), the two individuals can join in a covenant relationship as equals.

After the man affirms this gift from God, the author of Genesis 2 writes that in joining together in this covenant relationship they become one flesh. Though of course the first humans don't have parents, the assumption is that once two people come together they will leave the control of their parents and continue the journey together. In other words, the author of Genesis does interpret this as defining the nature of a marriage relationship. This statement about becoming one flesh has usually been interpreted in terms of entering a sexual relationship. In many cultures if two people do not consummate the marriage sexually, they are not considered married. On the other hand, in other cultures if you engage in sexual activity with another person then you are deemed to be married to them. Consider that even if Jacob didn't know that it was Leah who was sent into the tent with him; once they coupled sexually they were married (Genesis 29:21-27).

While the phrase "one flesh" can have sexual connotations and most cultures assume that a marriage will include sexual intimacy, that isn't necessarily true. In our American context it is the legal document, usually filed with a county clerk, that defines one as being married. What happens after that in the bedroom is no one's business.

When Paul calls on persons who experience a sexual attraction that isn't controllable to get married (1 Corinthians 7), he raises the question of whether or not there is a proper sphere for sexual activity. In our own culture, probably a majority of couples, especially younger ones, cohabit before they get married. Therefore, one would assume that they have been sexually active before marriage. Not everyone approves, of course, but as they say "the cat is out of the bag." In biblical times, they would probably already be considered married. To engage in sexual activity outside of marriage when one was already married was considered adultery. Now a man could have multiple wives, but a woman couldn't have multiple husbands. So in many ways it was the woman who faced judgment for committing adultery, not the man. On the other hand, reading through the Bible we find references to fornication, which is defined as promiscuous sexual activity. This too is condemned, but for different reasons. The culture in which the Scriptures were written were concerned about sexual behavior. The Scriptures set boundaries that serve as guides for proper sexual behavior. While these rules may have been developed to protect property rights, perhaps these rules can serve us as a reminder that sex should not be casual. Because it is an intimate relationship, in which two people share their bodies with each other, this should be done with great care.

The concept of "one flesh" that is found here in Genesis 2 likely speaks of sexual intimacy, but is this the only way it can be understood? William Stacy Johnson believes that limiting the concept of "one flesh" to sexual intimacy is too narrow an interpretation. He suggests that the concept of becoming "one flesh" can refer to becoming "one family." The reference to leaving one's family of origin and joining with another is seen as shifting one's allegiance from one's family of origin to a new family.

> While the intensity of marital "cleaving" no doubt flows in part from the natural, erotic desire that exists between a man and a woman in love. Nevertheless, there is more to it than that, as the story of Ruth makes clear.[4]

---

4   William Stacy Johnson, *A Time to Embrace: Same-Sex Relationships in Religion, Law, and Politics,* 2nd edition, (Grand Rapids: Wm. B. Eerdmans Publishing Co., 2012), p. 151.

In the story of Ruth, a Moabite woman refuses to "leave" (*'azab*) behind her mother-in-law, and insists on "cleaving" (*dabaq*) to Naomi. This isn't a sexual relationship, but it is a transition in familial relationships. The question then is this—must every family relationship involve a man and a woman, or could there be other forms, some of which do not involve sexual intimacy? If we follow Johnson's interpretation could a same-gender relationship, one that is possibly sexual in nature, express this idea of being one flesh?

Now, if we interpret Genesis 2 to refer to the necessity of human companionship, that doesn't mean that marriage is the only way in which this need for companionship can be fulfilled. One can be single and experience community in a variety of ways that do not need to be sexual in nature. This is an important issue for the church, because putting an emphasis on marriage can suggest to single people that they are somehow less human than those who are married. Married life is not normative. As we have this conversation about marriage, we want to refrain from suggesting that we are a collection of "pairs and spares." Genesis 2 suggests the human need for community. But is there only one way in which community can be understood?

In asking these questions we do so in a changing cultural context, where the larger society has broadened the options available to persons. Until quite recently it was assumed by our society that the only appropriate manifestation of marriage and family should involve persons of the opposite sex. That is no longer true, as polling even before the Supreme Court overturned bans on same-sex marriage, showed that a growing majority of Americans supported gay marriage. The Supreme Court ruling simply affirmed this trend in opinion by setting up a new legal definition of marriage that would treat same-sex and opposite-sex couples equally. What affect then do these changing cultural realities have on Christian understandings of gender, marriage, and our reading of texts like Genesis 2?

When we read Genesis 2, does the fact that the two people involved in this first coupling are of the opposite gender mean that this is the only possible form of coupling allowed by God? That is, must we understand "fitness" of the partner to be gender specific? Many interpreters would say yes to this question, but what if the person you are attracted to is the same gender? Could this mean that this person of the same gender is the partner most fit for you? If this is true, then, is this person with whom you would want to enter a life-long covenant relationship? There is a growing number of interpreters who suggest that this is the best way of reading this passage.

The issue here is one of particularity. Does the fact that when the biblical authors speak of something we understand to be marriage, they speak in terms of male-female relationships, mean that this is the only possible pattern? Are we limited by social norms present among those who gave us the biblical story? After all, in the Hebrew Bible there are a number of persons living in polygamous marriages. That the culture has apparently changed by the first century doesn't mean that official rules against polygamy were issued.

While marriage is culturally defined, and what constitutes a marriage today may be different from what we find in the Bible, it is important to have a definition of marriage. Even if we expand the definition to include same-gender relationships, we need to have some agreement on what it is we're talking about. Many are concerned that by expanding the definition, we're redefining marriage. That needn't be so. I appreciate the definition offered by Gerald Schlabach, who notes that marriage "is the communally sealed bond of lifelong intimate mutual care between two people that creates humanity's most basic unit of kinship, thus allowing human beings to build sustained networks of society."[5] Definitions are important. Schlabach offers us a good foundation for further discussion. While procreation remains part of the equation, it's not the only part. It does, however, normally include "tender other-directed sexual pleasuring." He continues by noting that "such

---

5   Gerald Schlabach, "What Is Marriage Now? A Pauline Case for Same-Sex Marriage," *The Christian Century,* (October 29, 2014), Vol. 31, No. 22, p. 24.

pleasure bonds a couple by promising and rewarding all the other ways of being together in mutual care and service through days, years, and decades."[6]

This is a question that remains under discussion. My own feeling is that what is said here of a male-female partnership, could be said of committed covenanted same-gender relationships. The particularity of the language in the Bible reflects cultural norms. Those norms are changing; so should we change with them?

A CALL TO REFLECTION AND CONVERSATION

1. What are reasons why people get married in our culture?
2. In the Genesis 2 story of creation, God creates the man and sees that it is not good that he is alone. What does this story say to us about the importance of community?
3. In what ways does marriage provide a foundation for companionship? What are other ways in which people can find fit companions?
4. What does the man mean by calling the woman "bone of my bone and flesh of my flesh"? How does this recognition come to fulfillment in the call to become one flesh?
5. Based on the reading of Genesis 2, how might same gender relationships fulfill this need for a fit companion? Is this different from heterosexual couples? Why or why not?

A CALL TO ACTION

Find wedding pictures and share them in the small group. As you look at the pictures ask how these pictures reflect the sense that the two partners are finding in each other fit companions for the journey of life.

A CALL TO PRAYER

> *Creator of everything good and perfect, when you saw that the man was lonely and incomplete, you created from*

---

6   Schlabach, "What is Marriage Now?" pp. 24-25.

him a companion fit for him. We who have a holy longing for human companionship pray that you would open our eyes to those who share flesh of our flesh and bone of our bone, finding in one another companions for the journey. And if those companions should become partners in marriage, may these partnerships express joy and thanksgiving.

CHAPTER 3

FIT COMPANIONS? WHAT IF I'M SINGLE?

1 Corinthians 7:1-7, 32-35

In the movie *Cast Away*, which hearkens back to Defoe's *Robinson Crusoe*, Tom Hanks' character Chuck Noland survives being stranded on a deserted island in large part because he imprinted personhood on a volleyball, whom he named Wilson (after the brand of volleyball). The movie raises important questions about the ways in which we develop relationships and how these relationships sustain us.

If according to Scripture it isn't good for human beings to be alone—the apparent message of Genesis 2—then we need companions in life to be emotionally, spiritually, and physically healthy. As we've seen, from the perspective of the author of Genesis 2, neither the divine-human relationship nor relationships with other animal species—no matter how much people may love their cats or their dogs—resolves humanity's deep-rooted need for community. While marriage is certainly one way in which this aloneness can be addressed, is this the only way in which full human community can be experienced? While the church often emphasizes "marriage and family," can one remain single and still find true community? If so, what form does this community take?

Until quite recently it has been the assumption of the broader culture that most people at some point will get married, and that this marriage will involve a man and a woman. Today not only is society's understanding of who can get married changing, but so is the expectation that a fulfilled life will include getting married. In recent years many couples are choosing to delay marriage until they get settled into a career and others are simply choosing not to get married (in spite of the legal benefits accrued to them by marriage). In part this is due to the feeling that marriage is a flawed institution that provides no guarantees of stability or happiness. If half of marriages end in divorce, then why bother getting married in the first place? While marriage patterns are in flux, growing numbers of Americans are not to coupling up at all.

Some people simply don't want to get married. They enjoy the freedom that singleness brings. Others simply never find the right partner. Others may have been married, but now find themselves single due to either the death of a spouse or divorce. There are those who choose the single life in order to devote themselves to a career or to service to others. This has been foundational to monasticism, which usually assumes that the monastic will be celibate. The question then is, how does one who is single experience human intimacy (whether or not this intimacy is in some way sexual in nature)?

It has been assumed by many, at least in Christian circles, that to be single was to be celibate. Therefore, whatever form intimacy might take, it was to be expressed within prescribed boundaries of sexual propriety. In many cultures, men have had more freedom to engage in sexual encounters outside of marriage than women, the reasons being varied depending on the culture. One reason being that women, not men, get pregnant. With various forms of birth control available today, many of which are both safe and effective, women have greater freedom sexually than in earlier ages. The so-called "sexual revolution" has been linked to the ready legal availability of the "pill," which became available to women in the mid-1950s. With the ready availability of contraception women could join men in experiencing sexual intimacy outside of the traditional boundaries. Contraception has proven to be the great equalizer, both inside and outside marriage.

While the older mores have relaxed considerably, the assumption that sex and marriage go together has remained largely in place (even if not always observed). For a variety of reasons, the old rules are being questioned within the Christian community. If sex and procreation have been separated, then the focus becomes the nature of human intimacy. From a Christian perspective, what is appropriate? As Christian Piatt reminds us, "as sexual beings, all of us struggle to channel our desires in healthy, constructive ways."[7]

For many the question of sex is not an appropriate one for polite Christians to engage in, which means that faith often doesn't play a role in contemporary conversations. That feeling has begun to change as the debate over same-sex marriage has raised questions of propriety, even as the debate has overshadowed the sexual revolution that is going on within the church.

We don't often talk about it publicly, but growing numbers of church members are sexually active and living together without benefit of clergy. Many couples are delaying marriage, but choosing to live together in the interim. Regarding this group, should we consider them single or already *de facto* married, even if the legal papers haven't been signed and the ceremony hasn't taken place? Remember that even though Jacob thought he was marrying Rachel, once he consummated the relationship with Leah they were married. What about the growing numbers of senior citizens who have lost their spouses, and seek companionship without getting married so as not to lose their full Social Security benefits?

Whatever the reason for choosing not to get married, is there a place for those who are single to experience sexual intimacy, even if these relationships are temporary? As we consider this question, we might ask whether our more casual view of sex underestimates the degree to which a sexual encounter, even between friends who aren't choosing to be together permanently, changes the nature of a relationship so that remaining friends is extremely difficult if not impossible. In regards to the way sexual intimacy affects relationships, Lewis Smedes wrote:

> The physical intimacy—two uncovered bodies entangled in closeness, one entering the very body of the others that sex belongs only where the two *persons* are very close and committed. The orgasm—two people out of their senses in ecstatic

---

7   Christian Piatt, *Post Christian: What's Left, Can We Fix It, Do We Care,* (New York: Jericho Books, 2014), *p.* 79.

abandon—hints for most people at the need for trust, for confidence that such self-giving out to be matched by a self-giving
of the persons. And the memory—two people who have slept
with each other never again see each other through the same
eyes—hints that nothing which happens between two people
can compare in depth with sexual intercourse.[8]

Since the cultures in which Scripture emerged were so different from our modern cultures, there is little to found that directly
speaks to our situation. The idea of dating would be foreign to our
ancestors. So, we will have to look at this more indirectly, perhaps
starting with the premise that we are called to love our neighbors
as we love ourselves. Therefore, simply engaging in sex recreation-
ally, with no recognition of the emotional side of the sexual act
is not loving or just. Thus, engagement in sexual relationships
need, whether inside or outside of marriage, to follow some basic
principles that respect each other. Margaret Farley suggests that
these principles include consent, mutuality, and equality. But surely
there is more than this for Christians? Therefore, she adds to these
principles that of commitment, even covenant.[9] This is a conversation that will need to continue, but it will require that the church
become more open in its conversations about sexuality.[10]

Early Christianity was a bit ambivalent about marriage. Paul
believed that celibacy was the most profitable state of Christian life.
His vision was both missional and apocalyptic. In 1 Corinthians 7
it's clear that Paul believes that the end of the age is at hand, and

8   Lewis B. Smedes, *Mere Morality: What God Expects from Ordinary People,*
    (Grand Rapids: Wm. B. Eerdmans Publishing Company, 1983), p. 166.
9   Margaret Farley, *A Framework for Christian Sexual Ethics,* (New York:
    Continuum Books, 2006), pp. 216-226.
10 The discussion of propriety of sex outside of marriage continues un-
    abated. Farley's admittedly scholarly exposition of a sexual ethic that is
    both just and loving provides groundwork for this, though she expects
    fidelity within marriage. David Gushee has written an important text on
    inclusion of LGBT Christians in the church, and in doing so argues for
    the importance of restricting sexual relationships to a covenant marriage,
    thus extending marriage to gay and lesbian partners. See David Gushee,
    Changing Our Mind, 2nd edition, (Canton, MI: Read the Spirit Books,
    2015), chapter 16.

therefore there is no need to marry and leave a legacy of family behind. With the end on the horizon it would be best to remain single and thus freed from concerns for family; a person was freed up for mission (1 Corinthians 7:32-35). This was Paul's ideal, an ideal that later took the form of monasticism, but Paul knew that not everyone was gifted in the same way as him. Therefore, if a person couldn't control their passions, then they should get married. To each is given a gift. To some is given the gift of celibacy.[11] If not, then marriage is the best solution to one's sexual needs. It seems so cut and dry, doesn't it?

If we read 1 Corinthians 7 in light of Paul's apocalyptic understandings, then we can understand why he puts no emphasis on the need to be married or to leave a legacy of children. While there are some who believe that we live at the end of time, the fact is the earth has continued to spin for nearly two thousand years since Paul wrote those words. We have settled in for the long haul, and that has led to the conclusion that it's appropriate to be married and even have children. We have returned to the normal patterns of human existence. Paul couldn't envision the Christian movement continuing to exist two thousand years after he wrote this letter. One generation was enough, but time has worn on and so people started getting married and having children. Otherwise the movement would have died out. It's instructive to consider the story of movements like the Shakers who practiced strict celibacy. Although they're still around, they're a fraction of their earlier glory. In large part that's because the movement's celibate members left no children or grandchildren.

Since we seem to no longer live under the shadow of this apocalyptic vision, a normalcy of family and children has set in. For the most part society has assumed that heterosexual marriage was the norm. Therefore, churches have tended to emphasize ministry to married couples and their families. What this means is that the

---

11   For a discussion of the gift of celibacy see Robert D. Cornwall, *Unfettered Spirit: Spiritual Gifts for the New Great Awakening*, (Gonzalez, FL: Energion Publications, 2013), pp. 135-136.

church is often a less than welcoming place for those who are single. Unless a person is called to a life of service and mission, the church isn't sure what to do with singles. Sometimes church members try to play matchmaker, or they cordon them off from the rest of the church, fearing that they could be potential predators or at the very least a temptation to stray.

With this backdrop of a non-apocalyptic normalcy, and the fact that twenty-first century realities differ markedly from the ancient world, at least in the West, what role will Scripture play in this conversation? We live in an age when marriage is delayed. Instead of marriages being arranged by families, we expect persons to date numerous others until they find the right mate, if that occurs. Added to all of this is the reality that women no longer need to depend on a man for protection and support, as was true for Naomi and Ruth when they arrived in Israel.

Remember that Naomi directed her daughter-in-law, Ruth, who was still young enough to bear children, to seek a match with Boaz, her nearest kinsman (Ruth 3). While it would appear that both Jesus and Paul were single, with Paul lifting it up as the preferred state of being in the world, they would probably have been outside the mainstream of society. Of course, while many find it difficult to consider the possibility posed by the Nikos Kazantzakis novel (and Martin Scorsese movie) *The Last Temptation of Christ* that Jesus might have been "tempted" by the ideas of marriage and sexual intimacy, we need to at least consider the possibility. After all, orthodox Chalcedonian Christianity has insisted that Jesus is not only fully divine, but fully human. Could Jesus have contemplated marriage and even sexual intimacy, as the Nikos Kazantzakis novel and Martin Scorsese film suggest? While the Gospels don't speak of such things, we can't rule out such ideas. It's possible that the Gospel writers simply didn't choose to tell us about such things, but even if he wasn't married, he was truly human.

Although the Gospels don't speak of Jesus being married, we do know from the Gospels that he had female friends, some of whom were very close to him. As for Paul, he deals with this question quite directly. As I noted earlier, in the seventh chapter of 1 Corinthians he addresses marriage, sexual intimacy, and celibacy. Many have interpreted this passage suggesting that Paul has a negative view of both marriage and sexual intimacy. The earliest editions of the New International Version, translated verse 1 of Chapter 7 as: "Now for the matters you wrote about: It is good for a man not to marry." More recent editions have brought the translation into line with current thinking, wherein the idea that a man should not touch a woman wasn't Paul's idea. Instead, this is what a certain group of Corinthian Christians had deemed appropriate if one wanted to be truly spiritual. This runs counter to the biblical story, which, as Mark Achtemeier points out "far from placing spirituality and sexuality in opposition, God is the inventor of sex in the scriptural account."[12]

Returning to this idea of giftedness, it is worth delving into Paul's thinking further. He sees this state as being a *charism*. While Paul may have had ascetic tendencies, he couches his statements about celibacy not only in the context of his apocalypticism, but also in his concern for the possibilities of ministry. To be single/celibate is to put oneself in a freer state for service.[13] While each has his or her own gift, Paul seems to suggest that his is a higher *charism* (1 Corinthians 7:7-8), and his emphasis on this will influence later developments, including the development of monasticism and priestly celibacy.

While Paul may have thought that celibacy was a higher calling, perhaps we can envision this idea of giftedness somewhat differently. Is it not possible to think of being either single or married as being a state of existence in which we can live in relationship with God and be blessed by that relationship? Neither marriage nor singleness should be lifted up as the divinely approved status. Perhaps these are two *charisms;* that is two different ways in which we can live in the Spirit. Although these two states of being differ

---

12   Mark Achtemeier, *The Bible's Yes to Same-Sex Marriage: An Evangelical's Change of Heart,* (Louisville: Westminster John Knox Press, 2014), p. 45.

13   Cornwall, *Unfettered Spirit,* pp. 135-136.

in many ways, we can live lives that allow blessed communion with God and with neighbor.

One could argue, as Paul does, that singleness is to be valued because it gives greater opportunity for undistracted work for God. It is true that one who is married must take into consideration the needs, desires, and welfare of his or her spouse before embarking on such a work, while the single person might not have the same kind of distractions (1 Corinthians 7:32-35). This does not make marriage bad and celibacy good, but for Paul, not having a family means being more available for God's mission. But, surely enforced celibacy can have detrimental effects on those who have a call to ministry but not celibacy.

In an age when being unmarried might have been frowned upon, this passage gives great freedom. Not everyone must be married or have children if they are to please God. By the same token, one can serve God and be married. If one chooses to be married, then this relationship will likely be fully sexual. Indeed, one need not practice sexual abstinence within marriage to experience a deeper connection with God. For Paul the important thing to remember is that in whatever situation one finds one's self, one should be available to God. But what if one is not married and not gifted for celibacy? That is the question we wrestle with. What is appropriate? What word of wisdom can we find in Scripture that can guide relationships that have either not reached a point of marriage or never will?

I will admit that this particular chapter/session was difficult to write. After all, I write this as one who has been married for over thirty years. It's been a long time since I experienced singleness. I was also raised with the assumption—even if this assumption was often ignored in practice—that sex should await marriage (we would debate the question of how far was too far). In addition, I write this as one who has officiated at numerous weddings, pronouncing divine blessings on these marriages. While I've looked to Genesis 2 as a word of wisdom for marriage—and the role that companionship plays in it—it needs to be made clear that there are many different ways in which this need for community can be fulfilled. When it comes to the community of faith, neither being married nor single is a higher calling.

A CALL TO REFLECTION AND CONVERSATION

1. How does one be single and experience true human community?
2. How does one experience human intimacy as a single person?
3. While it is assumed that marriage will include sexual intimacy, is it possible to experience sexual intimacy outside a covenant relationship? How does sexual intimacy affect one's relationships if not experienced within a covenant relationship?
4. How has the church received those who are single?
5. How might the church be more welcoming and nurturing to those are single?

A CALL TO ACTION

As a group consider ways in which the church can better minister with and those are single. Look at the programming life of the church. Where are their opportunities for singles to be involved? Look also at the ways in which the church encourages and supports true community for singles?

A CALL TO PRAYER

May the community of faith be a place of welcome so that no matter one's family status a caring home and a place of support might be found. In whatever state we find ourselves may we find spiritual sustenance in through the presence of the Spirit. Amen.

CHAPTER 4

HOW TO FIND A MATE (OR NOT)?

Hosea 1:2-9

How do people go about finding a mate in the twenty-first century? It is likely that younger generations might answer that question differently than earlier generations. The differences between today and the ancient world are even starker. While there are still places in the world where marriages are arranged by families, this would be a rare occurrence in North America. In our culture it is assumed that people will find their own mates. As a result, most people seeking a mate will date a number of people before making that "fateful" decision. This dating process might begin early in high school and continue for many years, until the day one either finds the right person or decides to end the search. In the course of this journey, people may discover that they are attracted to persons of the same gender. Whether one is gay or straight, it's assumed that a person needs to get to know a variety of people before concluding the search, even if the search ends relatively early in life.

Even after arriving at a decision, couples still have to decide whether to seal this relationship in a marriage ceremony. In our day there are increasing numbers of people who have decided that marriage as an institution is dead and therefore they will forgo its benefits (at least the ones accrued from the government). For those who choose to go the marriage route, growing numbers of people assume that it is not a life-time commitment. After all, many couples have emerged from homes where their parents were divorced. Since no one knows what the future will bring, at least for now they feel comfortable to join together in this legal bond called marriage. Because many couples are delaying marriage or remarrying, growing numbers of couples are creating pre-nuptial agreements to protect assets brought into the marriage, just in case something goes wrong. It's better to be safe than sorry.

Over the past thirty years, the median age at which couples enter a marriage for the first time has increased from 24.7 for males and 22.0 for women to 28.2 and 26.1 respectively in 2010. That might not seem like a lot at first glance, but a lot happens in four years time. One of the differences between that earlier day (around the time that Cheryl and I were married) and today is that the trend, especially among women, is to first get established in the work force and then begin looking to settle down, get married, and perhaps have children.

This decision to postpone getting married until one is established in one's career may explain the growing interest in internet dating sites, which range from secular to religious. If a person waits until they get established in a career, they likely will no longer be connected to the traditional places where mates were once discovered, places like high school and college. As a result, our television screens are filled with advertisements for dating sites such as *Match. com* and *eHarmony.com*, all promising that their specially designed software can help participants find that perfect match. They even tap into the vision that each person has a special soul mate. For Christians there are sites such as *ChristianMingle.com* that suggest God can use this site to help guide you to the perfect match. As they say on the website: "Trust God and your God-given instincts to guide you through this experience." All you have to do is create your profile, pay the fees, and you're on your way to finding the person God has for you. Besides, as more than one couple has told me, the internet is a better place to find a partner than a bar.

When we think about what Scripture might have to say about the way we find a mate, it is important to remember that marriages, at least for women, were entered into quite young, and were arranged by families. These arrangements often had strategic political or financial benefits. Women, as a general rule, were understood to be the property, first of the father and then of the husband, so in essence the wife was being bought and sold as a commodity. A father of a daughter needed to make sure that his investment in his daughter received the best return.

Of course, marriages weren't always completely commercial ventures. We can find romantic moments in the Bible. It also appears that there was true love between couples, but for the most part love came after the marriage and not prior to it. The idea, however, that one would go on a date—or even date different people before deciding whom to marry—would be a very foreign concept to the people we meet in Scripture. Therefore, the idea that the Bible can provide us with principles for dating makes little sense. It's not that there isn't some good moral advice to be found in Scripture, it's just not specific to dating. Yes, Jacob might have fallen in love with Rachel at the well, but he had to wait seven years before he could marry her, and he ended up with Leah before he got her.

While it was often said at my high school Bible study that we shouldn't be "unequally yoked with an unbeliever" (2 Corinthians 6:14), Paul probably wasn't talking about dating. The reason why we were encouraged to refrain from dating non-Christians was that dating outside the fold was considered risky. The idea of missionary dating—dating non-Christians with an eye to converting them—was especially discouraged. The word of wisdom shared with us was this—if Christ is going to be the center of your relationship, then it is wise to partner with someone who shares your faith in Christ. Otherwise things get tricky. However, many families are composed of people who at the very least share different Christian denominations, and many others two religious communities.[14]

So, how did people find a mate back in Bible times? Genesis is an excellent place to go for examples of how matches were made in the ancient world. Consider one example—the story of how Isaac got connected with Rebekah. In this story, Abraham was getting old and Sarah had already died. He needed to protect his

---

14 Robert LaRochelle, *A Home United*, (Gonzalez, FL: Energion Publications, 2015).

legacy. Remember that God had promised him that through the descendants of Isaac the nations would be blessed. Abraham didn't think that the local Canaanite women would make a good wife for Isaac (this won't be the last time that this happens). Concerned that Isaac needed to find a proper mate he called in his servant, and made him promise to go back to Abraham's people, and find a wife there for his son. There was one major stipulation. This future bride had to be willing to leave her home and join Isaac in their new country. There was no going back for Abraham and his descendants. With this charge from Abraham, the servant took ten camels, along with choice gifts, and headed off for the city of Nahor in Aram-na-haraim. Arriving in the appropriate neighborhood, the servant stopped at a well. Wells seem to have been a great place to meet eligible girls. So, having arrived at the local well, he settles down his camels, and prays to God for success in finding a mate for his master's son. He prays:

> *"Let the girl to whom I shall say, 'Please offer your jar that I may drink,' and who shall say, 'Drink, and I will water your camels'—let her be the one whom you have appointed for your servant Isaac. By this I shall know that you have shown steadfast love to my master."* (Genesis 24:14)

Before he finished the prayer, Rebekah, the daughter of Abraham's brother, came to the well. She responded appropriately to the servant's request that she give him a drink and water his camels. Therefore, he gave her a gold nose ring and two gold bracelets (that age's engagement ring?), and the deal was made. This couple who will play a significant role in the biblical story, never met until the servant brought her home to where Isaac was living. All that was left to do was for Isaac to take her into his mother's tent, and with that she became his wife. Only then, after the wedding, do we learn that "he loved her" (Genesis 24). As we saw earlier with Jacob and his two wives, the marriage was kept within the family. The bride and groom were first cousins, but apparently that was okay back then.

That is one story of matchmaking. There are many like it. Some matches are good. Some aren't. While Solomon is said to be wise, his choices in wives were roundly condemned. It seems he "loved many foreign women," including Pharaoh's daughter. As a result, he was led astray to worship the gods of his many wives (the danger of being unequally yoked). Of course, Solomon's marriages were probably based on strategic partnerships, of which the writers of 1 Kings didn't approve (1 Kings 11:1-10).

One of the more interesting matches is one that Yahweh instigated. God told the prophet Hosea to go and marry a prostitute. God says to Hosea "'Go take for yourself a wife of whoredom, and have children of whoredom, for the land commits great whoredom by forsaking the Lord.' So he went and took Gomer, daughter of Diblaim, and she conceived and bore him a son" (Hosea 1:2-3). She would bear him several children, all of whom were given horrific names at God's behest. They're horrific names because they speak of divine judgment. If anything, this story is a warning against saddling children with unflattering names. It also reminds us that marriages and families are often dysfunctional from the very beginning because they are built upon unfortunate foundations. We might think that God is involved in this, but is this really true?

When we read the biblical story, it seems clear that there isn't one universal pattern for choosing a partner. It's also clear that the patterns we find in the biblical story do not fit very well, if at all, with our current realities. While there are some attempts, among certain groups to retain older visions of women, in most of our communities, such a vision is not welcomed. The idea that a woman is the property of her father or her husband is simply repugnant to our modern sensibilities.

Scripture may not provide guidelines for modern matchmaking; it does suggest that there is more than one way to go about this part of life. Some of the stories, like that of the pairing of Isaac and Rebekah remind us that love can blossom even after a match is made. And perhaps the internet can be just as useful a tool as stopping by the local well—and likely much better than going to a

bar! The most important thing to remember is that even in changing times, the key is respecting the humanity of the other person.

A CALL TO REFLECTION AND CONVERSATION

1. If you are married or in a committed relationship, how did
you find your partner?

2. What is your opinion on internet dating sites? What are
the benefits and the challenges of such a site?

3. Some of these sites speak of finding the perfect match or
soul mate? What do you think of this idea?

4. As you looked into the biblical stories of marriage matches,
what do you take from them?

5. What role does your faith play in who you look for in a
possible life partner?

6. What do you think of the idea of being "unequally yoked?"
What are the challenges of being in a relationship with a person
who doesn't share your faith?

A CALL TO ACTION

As a group check out the various internet dating sights—
Match.com, eHarmony.com, ChristianMingle.com. What do these
sites say about how they match couples up with each other? What
are the criteria they use? Discuss what you find, including whether
you might turn to a site like this.

A CALL TO PRAYER

> *Lord Jesus Christ, who by your presence and power
> brought joy to the wedding at Cana: bless those engaged to be
> married, that there may be truth at the beginning of their lives
> together, unselfishness all the way, and perseverance to the end*
>
> *May their hopes be realized and their love for each oth-
> er deepen and grow, that through them your name may be
> glorified. Mother's Union. (The Complete Book of Christian
> Prayer, p. 80)*

CHAPTER 5

IT'S A COVENANT NOT A CONTRACT!

Ruth 1:16-18

When we look at marriage from the perspective of a secular government, it is essentially a binding contract entered into by two consenting parties and certified by the state. This contract brings with it certain obligations and privileges—including significant tax benefits (at least in the United States) unless you are seniors or disabled and on Social Security. The state provides these incentives, because it has been assumed that stable families—bound together with legally enforceable agreements—provide for a stronger community and nation. As Justice Anthony Kennedy declared in writing for the majority in *Obergefell v. Hodges,* which overturned bans on same-sex marriage, "this Court's cases and the Nation's traditions make clear that marriage is a keystone of our social order."[15] Because marriage is seen as a core value in the nation, the equal protection clause of the Fourteenth Amendment, requires that the right to marry be extended to same-sex couples.

As a legal contract, it continues indefinitely, unless the parties choose to end it through divorce proceedings. These marriage contracts can, and often are, celebrated with religious ceremonies. The ceremonies, however, are optional. The most important requirement is that the couple signs the document, has it witnessed by their representatives, along with another duly authorized person, often clergy, but not necessarily clergy, who act as agents of the state. Once this document has been filed with the local county clerk, the couple is married in the eyes of the state (and perhaps also in the eyes of God).

---

15   *Obergefell v. Hodges,* p. 16.

That definition of marriage may seem rather dry and me-
chanical, but essentially—from a governmental perspective—that's
what marriage is. And, for some, that's about all marriage is. It's
a contract that can be negated at any time by filing the proper pa-
perwork. After all, when the romance begins to fade, and another
person comes along who lights a fire, well then it may be time to
move on. We do it with cars and jobs, why not spouses? Of course
few people enter marriage with that attitude, but it is a temptation
all couples face, even those bound together in marriage.

If we look at marriage from a religious/spiritual perspective,
we might want to use a different kind of language. We might want
to speak of covenant rather than contract. On the surface it might
not seem like there's much difference, but theologically there is a
great difference. Instead of the state being the third party in the
relationship, God is the third party. The saying from Ecclesiastes
concerning a three-fold cord fits nicely here:

> *Again, if two lie together, they keep warm; but how can*
> *one keep warm alone? And though one might prevail against*
> *another, two will withstand one. A threefold cord is not quick-*
> *ly broken.* (Ecclesiastes 4:11-12)

If we understand marriage to be a covenant relationship, then
God provides that third thread or fold that creates a strong bond
between the two partners as they take their life journey together.
Although clergy often perform a governmental role by signing off
on a marriage license, this isn't the reason why the church and its
clergy are involved. While people without a connection to a church
may choose a church wedding or have clergy perform weddings
(I've done my share) simply because it's traditional, and not because
they expect God to be part of their marriage, placing the ceremony in a sacred context does call to attention the bigger picture of
covenant. Even if a couple is not fully engaged with the idea of
covenant, the church/clergy can bring this to their attention (as I
always do in the weddings I officiate at).

When we think of the way covenants are described in Scripture, we usually look to the covenants God makes with Noah, Abraham, and Moses. In each case God makes promises and lists certain expectations. In each case God is the initiator of the covenant. There is another covenant story, however, that has a bearing on this conversation. It is a covenant entered into by two humans, and it can serve for us as the basis of our reflection on what it means for two people to join in a covenant relationship through marriage.

This story is found in the Book of Ruth. Ruth is a Moabite woman who had married an Israelite, the son of Naomi. After Ruth's husband died, along with a secod son of Naomi who also had married a Moabite woman, Naomi decides to head back home. She tries to convince her two daughters-in-law to return to their own families. Naomi has nothing to offer these two younger women. She is a widow without support—as are these two women. Orpah tearfully agrees to Naomi's demand, but Ruth refuses. Instead, she pledges to stay with Naomi.

While Ruth's covenant language is spoken by a daughter-in-law to her mother-in-law, they speak to what it means to live in any covenant relationship. This includes marriage.

Ruth says to Naomi—**"Where you go, I will go; where you lodge I will lodge."** As a couple enters this covenant relationship they pledge to go on the journey of life together. Wherever they go, they will lodge together. That is, they will make a home together. Because we live in an increasingly mobile society, modern couples may have much in common with Abraham and Sarah, Zipporah and Moses. It is quite likely that couples will not end up where they start their lives.

My advice to couples is to be ready to go—together—wherever the Spirit of God leads. This is true, even if it means leaving behind mother and father. Indeed, it means "cutting the cord" with parents and tying the knot with each other. Andrew and Judith Lester offer this word of wisdom for couples:

> To have a "self" to give in marriage it is necessary for you
> to experience your "self" as distinct from the family with whom

you grew up. This process is called differentiation: distinguishing one's self from that of the parenting figures and separating from the emotional womb of that family. Differentiation is the process of knowing where the boundaries of one's self end and the boundaries of another begin.[16]

While the relationship between Ruth and Naomi is different from that of a married couple, the principle in play is the same. Ruth left home to go with Naomi. She had to have a good sense of self to do this. She knew where the boundaries between her family of origin and her new family lay. Therefore, Ruth says to Naomi— **"Your people shall be my people."**

In Ruth's case, she was leaving her own Moabite people and joining herself with Naomi's people, the nation of Israel. This involved a major break in loyalties. When two people are married, they usually aren't making as large a break from their family of origins as Ruth was, though when a marriage bridges ethnic or religious boundaries today something similar might occur. It can also occur in same-gender marriages, if one or both families reject a couple's marriage. In the best of circumstances, however, marriage brings together two families. It is, at its best, a merger of families. This is another sense of what it means when we speak of the two becoming one flesh. This commitment also signals the importance of community. As William Stacy Johnson puts it: "The institution of marriage serves a community-building function. It connects the new family formed by the mutual love of two people to a wider family, a community of the faithful to which the couple contributes and from which it draws strength."[17]

Ruth says to Naomi— **"Your God, [is] my God."** When Ruth left behind her people and joined herself to Naomi's people, she left behind the gods of her people and embraced the God of Israel. Again the contemporary situation relating to marriage may differ from Ruth's experience. And yet, maybe it doesn't. We are

---

16 Andrew D. Lester and Judith L. Lester, *It Takes Two: The Joy of Intimate Marriage,* (Louisville: Westminster John Knox Press, 1998), p. 32.

17 Johnson, *A Time to Embrace,* p. 142

witnessing an increasing number of cross-faith marriages, and this raises interesting questions about what binds a couple together. If a couple has children, the issue of religion becomes even more complicated.

In this story, Ruth adopted the religion of her mother-in-law. She traded her gods for Naomi's God. If God is part of the marriage relationship, and I believe that God can be, then a couple will need to have a conversation about the role of religion in their marriage and their family life. If they come from different faith traditions, they will need to decide whether they will celebrate both traditions or just one of them. Of course, some couples decide to find a new faith community that seems to blend the two together in a way that is comfortable to both. There is a reason, of course, why cultures have frowned on inter-religious marriages. They can destabilize the family and therefore the community at large.

Writing to a newly forming church where one spouse may have adopted the Christian faith, and the other hadn't, Paul's counsel was not to seek a divorce, because the difference "for the unbelieving husband is made holy through his wife, and the unbelieving wife is made holy through her husband." On the other hand, if the unbelieving partner wished to leave, then the believer should not stand in the way of the separation (1 Corinthians 7:12-16). Interestingly, Paul doesn't suggest that this is divinely inspired advice; it's just his own common sense advice. There is then, no right or wrong way. Each case is different and needs to be treated pastorally within the church.

"Where you die, I will die—there I will be buried." Ruth tells Naomi: "I'm with you till the end. Where you are buried, that's where I will be buried." One of the traditional vows couples make to each other is that they commit themselves to each other until death separates them. As we will see in another session, not every marriage will make it to the end. This is a reality of human life, but the commitment that one makes in marriage is to remain together until death takes one or the other of the partners. The good news, the news that sustains even when covenants break, is that nothing, not even death can separate us from the love of God who sustains us on the journey.

What makes the covenant marriage different from the covenant relationship that Ruth and Naomi entered into was the sexual component. As the story of Ruth demonstrates, when Ruth and Naomi reach Naomi's homeland, she is directed to find a husband among Naomi's family. As the story continues, it is Boaz who will enter into that relationship. This covenant relationship that two people enter into is cemented in the sexual embrace. Lewis Smedes notes:

> A marriage is a covenanted partnership between two people who give themselves to one another in committed love. We call it a covenant for two reasons. First, it is created by the free wills of the people who make it and lasts as long as those wills determine. . ... Second, marriage is meant to be a personal life-sharing union; what marks it is the unreserved sharing of two human lives. The life-sharing of a covenant makes it different from a contract; a contract calls for an exchange of goods and services, and can be cancelled as soon as the arrangement is completed. The essence of covenant is different; it is the wholeness of life-sharing, not merely an exchange of goods and services to meet the needs and desires of the partners.[18]

The Seventh Commandment, the prohibition of adultery, comes into play here because adultery involves a breaking of the covenant. It is treating the other person as simply a provider of goods and services and not a person with whom one is wholly committed to.

It is sometimes said that marriage is nothing more than a piece of paper. In legal, contractual terms that may be true. In covenant-making terms it is much more.

A Call to Reflection and Conversation

1. What is a covenant?
2. How is marriage a covenant relationship?

---

18 Smedes, *Mere Morality*, p. 165.

3. How might the principles found in the story of Ruth and Naomi, the covenant statement that is often used at weddings, provide a foundation for marriage?

4. How is a covenant relationship different from a contractual one?

5. How does the sexual relationship within marriage express the covenant-making process?

6. How is adultery an act of breaking covenant?

A Call to Action

Using Bible study resources explore the idea of covenant in the Bible. In what ways is covenant described and expressed in both Testaments? How do these conversations about covenant speak to the marriage relationship?

A Call to Prayer

Gentle and loving God, may these two people, now married, keep this covenant they have made. May they be a blessing and comfort to each other, sharing each other's joys, consoling one another in sorrow, helping each other in all the changes of life. May they encourage each other in whatever they set out to achieve. May they, trusting each other, trust life, and not be afraid. We pray for them happiness . . . not freedom from life's struggles, but the knowing awareness that they are not alone. May they continue to love one another forever. Amen. (Chalice Worship, p. 44)

CHAPTER 6

SEX AND MARRIAGE GO TOGETHER

Song of Songs 7:10-13; 8:5-7

In the first creation story, after God created humankind as both male and female, God told them to be "fruitful and multiply" (Genesis 1:28). This command implies that sexual intimacy is part of the human experience. In the second creation story we are told that "a man leaves his father and his mother and clings to his wife, and they become one flesh." While the reference to becoming "one flesh" does not necessarily imply sexual intimacy—it could suggest the merging of families—it has traditionally had that implication. When we talk of marriage, there is an assumption that sexual intimacy will be part of the relationship (although some late in life marriages may not be sexual in nature).

When we think about sexual intimacy we could start from a strictly biological perspective. From the perspective of biology, sex is a normal part of the human experience. While not everyone will enter a sexual relationship, it is truly a part of being human. Not only is sex the means by which humans normally procreate (we must recognize the possibility of processes such as in vitro fertilization), it also provides the opportunity for two people to experience mutual pleasure. As the title of a popular Christian sex manual that has been around for decades puts it, sex is *Intended for Pleasure.* It is quite likely that the pleasuring part has evolutionary origins. If sex wasn't a pleasurable experience, then it's likely that humans would forgo it, which would lead to the demise of the human race. Therefore, while sexual relations between a man and a woman can lead to pregnancy, that needn't be the reason two people enter into a sexually intimate relationship.

We know that marriage isn't a necessary requirement for either engaging in sexual behavior or procreating. People have sex outside of marriage, even when societies have taboos against it. While contemporary sexual mores seem looser than in previous decades, it's not like human beings just discovered that they didn't have to get married to have sexual experiences. The Bible is full of stories of people who were involved sexually outside the bounds of marriage—consider for instance the stories of David and Bathsheba and Judah and Tamar. While both sets of relationships seemed to break the rules, yet the stories are still there. In fact, Tamar is found to be in the right, because her father-in-law failed to provide her with a husband who could produce a child with her. In the contemporary context the question isn't what society at large considers appropriate, but rather what should Christians consider to be appropriate?

The traditional "rules" governing sexual behavior have generally applied to women rather than men. Rarely will you see a man charged with adultery in Scripture, unless he is involved with someone else's wife. Remember the woman caught in adultery in John 8? Where was her partner? Why wasn't he brought before Jesus as well? But, as we've seen, in the ancient world, women were often understood to be property. A woman who had sex outside of a prescribed relationship was considered spoiled property. We don't think of women as property anymore—or at least I hope we don't—nor see their "value" as diminished by being sexually active outside of marriage.

As we read the biblical stories that speak of relationships that have the character of marriage, we need to remember that the ancients believed that the relationship between husband and wife was an unequal one. Ironically, most same-sex relationships in the Greco-Roman world were also of an unequal nature, and likely exploitive. Thus, when we read prohibitions against same-sex relationships in Scripture we need to remember that the authors weren't talking about a partnership of equals, any more than they did so with regard to male-female relationships.

One of the questions that influenced the development of Christian views of sexuality emerged out of conflicting understandings of the relationship of sexuality and spirituality. Many of the prohibitions in the Bible were written with the practices of rival religions in mind, wherein sex was used as a talisman to encourage the gods to bless the land with fertility. It wasn't just children, it was the flocks and the crops as well. At the same time, there have been faith groups that have believed that sexuality and spirituality were incompatible, because sex was considered too carnal and earthy. For Western Christians, our views of sexuality and the spiritually life tend to be influenced by Augustine and his story told in the *Confessions.*

For Augustine, sex was an expression of the flesh and marked the fall from a higher spiritual state. While humans might be equipped for sex from the beginning, it is better not to be so engaged. The act itself wasn't sinful, but it was always accompanied by the sin of sensuality and/or self-love.[19] Even when we assume that sex is part of marriage, even there we have seen it as somehow being carnal and even dirty. At one time men are supposed to like it, but women were expected to endure it, not enjoy it. For a woman to enjoy sex was to mark her as somehow being a loose woman. This understanding of sex that has been so influential over the years is given voice in this prayer offered by St. Augustine in the *Confessions.*

> Truly it is by continence that we are made as one and regain that unity of self which we lost by falling apart in the search for a variety of pleasures. For a man loves you so much the less if, besides you, he also loves something else which he does not love for your sake. O Love ever burning, never quenched! O Charity, my God, set me on fire with your love! You command me to be continent. Give me the grace to do as you command, and command me to do what you will![20]

---

19 See the discussion in James William McClendon, *Systematic Theology: Ethics,* (Nashville: Abingdon Press, 1986), p. 143-146.

20 Augustine, *Confessions (Penguin Classics),* R.S. Pine-Coffin, trans., (New York: Penguin Books, 1961), p. 233.

Therefore, a spiritual person would want to avoid such corruption, and embrace celibacy. Such views whether inspired by Gnosticism or Augustine have given support to the development of monastic and priestly celibacy. While Augustine is an important contributor to this vision, we can find it already present in the early church. Consider the conversation Paul has with a group of Christians in the Corinthian Church. Certain members of that community had gotten it in their head that true spirituality required sexual abstinence (1 Corinthians 7:5). This was true, they believed, whether one was married or not. However, some of the church members found it difficult to live up to this understanding of spirituality, and had begun acting in ways that were unbecoming to the community. It appears that they may have sought sexual satisfaction outside of the marriage relationship (perhaps by visiting local prostitutes).

While there seem to be numerous taboos, rules, and regulations concerning sexual behavior that would suggest that biblical writers and many early Christians were rather cool to the idea of sex, whether inside or outside marriage, there are, however, contrarian views that celebrate the joy of sex. One book that celebrates sex is the *Song of Songs*, though many Christians, including Augustine, have read this book allegorically so that Christians might experience its spiritual message and not be brought down to the carnal level.

We begin again with the premise that marriage will normally involve a sexual relationship. In the First Testament at least, the act of sleeping together was understood to be sufficient for a marriage to be consummated. Remember the story of Jacob and Leah. Jacob might protest that the woman he slept with (Leah) was not the woman he intended to marry (Rachel), but since he slept with Leah, she was his wife. One of the reasons for this is that a woman was considered property, and if she had slept with a man, not her husband, or was rejected by a prospective husband, then she would be spoiled or damaged goods. A man could sow his seeds with relative impunity, but once a woman had been with a man she essentially belonged to him. At least in western culture most people do not view women in quite the same way (one would hope). Though there are still elements of this understanding present in subtle forms, so that men are still freer to be sexually active outside marriage than are women.

The *Song of Songs* (*Song of Solomon* or *Canticles*) celebrates embodied love. While it can be read allegorically to speak of the human-divine relationship, to do so may cause us to miss its primary point, which is the beauty of embodied human love.

Consider these words from Song of Songs 7 that allow the woman to speak of her beloved: "I am my beloved's, and his desire is for me." In this statement she celebrates the mutual attraction that binds the couple together. Seemingly out of step with the culture, the woman also takes the lead in the relationship. She invites her beloved to walk through the fields and the gardens, where life is lush and fruitful, to a place where she says "There I will give you my love" (Song of Songs 7:10-12). The sharing of love here is physical. This is an expression of *eros,* which Thomas Oord defines as a form of love that "affirms what is good, beautiful, and valuable in creatures or in God."[21] The woman sees something good and valuable in the man, and she pursues it in a way that enhances his value to her. While she intends to show him a good time, this isn't a momentary fling.

In the chapter that follows, the woman sings of becoming the "seal upon your heart." She wants to be part of his very identity. Stephanie Paulsell writes that "the image of the marked or inscribed heart in the Hebrew Bible often points to deep knowledge, and a profound belonging." We see this expressed in Jeremiah 31:31-34, where Jeremiah speaks of the Law being inscribed on the heart rather than on tablets of stone. Such is the nature of the covenant that the woman seeks to share in with the one she pursues.[22]

---

21 Thomas Jay Oord, *The Nature of Love: A Theology,* (St. Louis: Chalice Press, 2010), p. 121.
22 Harvey Cox and Stephanie Paulsell, *Lamentations and the Song of Songs (Belief: A Theological Commentary),* Louisville: Westminster John Knox Press, 2012), p. 267.

So intertwined is this couple that the relationship, consummated sexually, is as strong as death. According to this scriptural author, it is a "passion fierce as the grave" (*Song of Songs* 8:6). In comparing the sexual relationship with the grave, it is clear that it is something not to be taken lightly—it demands everything of us. In traditional wedding vows, couples often pledge themselves to share life together "until death do us part." It is a covenant that invites the couple to be steadfast in their commitment to one another. Life may not go on forever, but it would appear that love pursues us beyond the grave. Again there is a word of wisdom offered by Paulsell that emerges from this passage. She notes the man is overwhelmed by the presence of the woman, but he also welcomes it. As for the woman, Paulsell writes:

> The risks the woman takes to be with her beloved cause her to be focused, not anxious. She knows the risks of loving, of course. She knows that love is not something to handle casually, and she counsels us throughout the poem not to awaken love prematurely. She advises us not to rush into love, but she does not teach us to be afraid of it.[23]

Remember how Paul warns that "it is better to marry than burn with passion?" (1 Corinthians 7:9 CEB). For Paul, marriage is the proper vehicle for satisfying the passion that burns within human beings to be joined in intimate embrace. Speaking of himself, however, he celebrates the possibility of being freed from these passions so that he (and others) can pursue God's mission in the world. Paul may celebrate the freedom entailed by celibacy, but such is not the case for the singer of this song. She declares that love is like a "raging flame" that is so powerful, that "many waters cannot quench love, neither can floods drown it" (Song of Songs 8:7).

You can understand why Augustine and others, who placed celibacy on a higher plane of life, would allegorize these words and apply them to the relationship with God. If God is to be the focus of our lives, then to be so consumed by another would take away

---

23 Cox and Paulsell, p. 268.

from one's relationship with God. The writer of this song, however, isn't worried about this occurring and instead celebrates the power that *eros* has over human beings.

The power of the sexual relationship raises questions about how one expresses oneself sexually. In "biblical times" it was assumed that one should not, or at least a woman should not, be sexually active outside of marriage. Adultery was deemed contrary to the Law of God. It was a form of breaking a covenant relationship. While earlier societies held women more responsible for sexual purity than they did for men, one would hope that today the call to fidelity in marriage would apply to both men and women. What makes things different today is that there is a growing sense that sex is as much about pleasure as it is about procreation, especially since contraception (as well as in vitro fertilization and even adoption) allows us to separate the sexual relationship from procreation. Contraception has essentially "liberated" modern people to be freer with their sexual experiences. Indeed, today sexually transmitted diseases are a greater concern than pregnancy for sexually active couples. Therefore, there is a growing sense that knowing where and when to be sexually intimate is a personal decision, even among those within the Christian community. At the same time, Christian teaching affirms the call to fidelity within the covenant relationship. As Nathan Maddox notes, "practicing fidelity to the marriage covenant involves being defined in relationship to our will rather than our feelings. This may be an unpopular statement in a culture and time when a premium is paid to feelings, but life and religious faith are about more than feelings."[24]

Our assumption here is that embodied love is central to the marriage relationship, and that fidelity to the covenant makes this possible. As we have already seen *Song of Songs* celebrates embodied love, and thus the human body. It is not a Gnostic sort of book

---

24 Nathan Mattox, "'A Wild Ass at Home in the Wilderness': Fidelity and the Life of Faith in a Hypersexualized, Consumer-driven Culture," in *Oh God, Oh God, Oh God! Young Adults Speak Out about Sexuality & Christian Spirituality,* Heather Godsey and Lara Blackwood Pickrel, eds., (St. Louis: Chalice Press, 2010), p. 105.

(unless we choose to allegorize it in such a way that it loses contact with its original context). The writer of the song goes into great detail describing the bodies of the two lovers, making it one of the most erotic poems to emerge in the ancient world. Remarkably, considering the sometimes puritanical nature of the Christian community (thank you Augustine), it is found in our Bibles. While we know it's there, we may quote from parts of it. But too often we forget how explicit the language gets. With that in mind it is important that we hear these words:

> *While the king was on his couch,*
> *my nard gave forth its fragrance.*
> *My beloved is to me a bag of myrrh*
> *that lies between my breasts.*
> *My beloved is to me a cluster of henna blossoms*
> *in the vineyards of Engedi.*
>
> (Song of Songs 1:12-14)

While we might not see the analogy in quite the same way, the groom describes the bride's beauty in very agrarian fashion. Her eyes are like doves, her hair like "goats moving down the slopes of Gilead." Her teeth are like a "flock of shorn ewes" and her "two breasts are like two fawns, twins of a gazelle, that feed among the lilies." And on it goes (Song of Songs 4:1-8). So, if you're into banning erotic books from the local library, you had better ban the Bible!

Because sexuality is such a powerful force it can be abused and misused. There is a reason why cultures have placed boundaries on the way in which people have expressed themselves sexually. The possibility of pregnancy was an important reason for setting up boundaries, but from a spiritual perspective, sex is more than a physical act. The sexual act has the potential to bind two people together in a way that no other act can. Once you have engaged in a sexual relationship with another, your relationship with that person will never be the same. This makes the idea of being "friends with benefits" problematic. Having become intimate with another person, at least one of the persons involved will form a deep emotional connection (and it's not necessarily a woman), which will change the nature of the relationship.

Fidelity is, as we noted earlier, a matter of the will, not feelings. Feelings for one another can ebb and flow with time. We may feel drawn to another person, so our ability to remain faithful will require an act of the will. In this case the slogan "if it feels good, do it" does not hold.

When it comes to relationships, they often begin with *eros*. *Eros* defines one person's desire for the other. It is an expression of love that is reflected in the readings from *Song of Songs*. *Eros* plays an important role in a marriage, but as I like to remind couples in wedding homilies, it is not sufficient to sustain a marriage. Therefore, it is important to rekindle this part of the relationship over time, but this too requires an act of the will. Yes, romance is important. Physical intimacy is important. But it is not the whole of marriage.

A successful marriage requires the couple to nurture a second form of love known in the Greek as *philia*. This word speaks of cooperative friendship and companionship. Marriages succeed when the two persons like each other. You have to want to be together and share life's bounty together outside the bedroom. It's not uncommon to speak of one's partner as one's best friend. This is a rather modern view, but it assumes that it will be one's spouse, who is there in all of life's ups and downs. This is what it means to be friends.

There is a third word for love, one that I often lift up in a marriage ceremony. That form is known as *agape*. We often speak of *agape* as being "unconditional love." It is similar to the Hebrew *hesed*, which is often translated as "steadfast love." In the Hebrew Bible we hear God declare that no matter what the people do, God will stand with them in "steadfast love." These are important nuances, but I also like the way theologian Tom Oord defines *agape* as "in spite of love." Some will remember the line from the movie *Love Story*—"love means never having to say you're sorry." The reality is that we humans are imperfect creatures, and we will, given time and opportunity, hurt each other. There will be times when we will have to say "I'm sorry." There will be the need for reconciliation—even in the best of marriages.

Marriage involves embodiment. It involves a physical element. The way in which that physicality is expressed may change over time. As we age, that physicality may be more expressed in things like kisses and hand holding, than it is through frequent sexual intercourse. But however it is expressed, touch is important. That touch, however, needs to be expressed in concert with friendship and unswerving commitment to the other. Tom Oord speaks of love being both intentional and responsive.[25] When it comes to the physical, the *eros* part of the relationship, it is an act of wasteful self-surrender on behalf of another. And as Paul makes clear in his letter to the Corinthian church, this relationship should be one of equals. He tells this community that "the husband should give to his wife her conjugal rights, and likewise the wife to the husband. For the wife does not have authority over her own body, but the husband does; likewise, the husband does not have authority over his own body, but the wife does" (1 Corinthians 7:3-4).

A CALL TO REFLECTION AND CONVERSATION

1. How does society as a whole view sex? Is this different or similar to the way the Christian faith/community understands sex?

2. From reading Scripture how is sex understood within the biblical story? How should we translate that into our own time and experience?

3. How should we understand the relationship of sex to spirituality?

4. How is sexual intimacy related to the marriage relationship?

5. The readings from *Song of Songs* seem to celebrate sexual intimacy. What do you take from these passages? How should they influence our understandings?

---

25   Thomas Jay Oord, *The Nature of Love: A Theology*, (St. Louis: Chalice Press, 2010), pp. 17, 56.

6. What differences do you see between the *Song of Songs* and the way Augustine views sexual intimacy?

A Call to Action

Churches struggle with talking seriously about sex, leaving their people, especially children and youth without any real guidance about sexuality from a Christian perspective. Therefore, either as a group or individually do a search for and if possible review religiously based sex education curriculum. Ask whether the materials are tied into Christian theology, tradition, and readings of Scripture. With the latter, is the use of Scripture primarily proof-texting or serious engagement with the text? Is the curriculum realistic or overly idealistic? Would you recommend its use in your congregation?

A Call to Prayer

God you created us with bodies that find pleasure through sexual intimacy. It is a gift to be treasured and honored. Guide us we pray that we might be good stewards of this gift, sharing life together in mutuality and love. Amen.

CHAPTER 7

MARRIAGE – A PARTNERSHIP OF EQUALS

2 Corinthians 7:1-7

The Bible came into being in a patriarchal age. Women were, for the most part, considered property—first of their fathers and then of their husbands. Although this vision may be the dominant position in the biblical story, there are alternative perspectives present in the Bible. At several points in the story women play either a leading role or have strong roles. Sarah, Deborah, Tamar, Miriam, Rahab, Ruth, and Naomi, to name but a few, play leading roles in the Hebrew Bible. Then there is in the New Testament the way in which Jesus engages with women and raises them up to the status of disciples. Consider that he makes his first resurrection appearance to Mary Magdalene and speaks to Mary of Bethany as a disciple. Although Paul is often viewed as less open to women leaders, he considers women such as Priscilla, Phoebe, and Junia as leaders in the church.

There are texts, such as 1 Corinthians 14, that command women to be silent and yet there are also passages that seem to overturn such a view. Indeed, in 1 Corinthians 11, even as he gives instructions for proper decorum in the church Paul assumes that women will be praying and prophesying in the church. When it comes to marriage relationships, Ephesians 5 can be interpreted in either hierarchical or egalitarian ways. At the heart of the debate over how to interpret these passages is the question of authority. Who, some may wonder, is going to be in charge? This question of authority is in some ways part of the dilemma posed by gay marriage. If the partners in the marriage are of the same gender, how do you decide who is in charge? For many in ancient and modern society the idea of equal partners, at least in marriage, is difficult to fathom.

For much of Christian history the question of authority has assumed that the husband/male is the head of the household. In fact, this vision stood at the very center of the doctrine of divine right monarchy. The monarchy simply reflected the household, which of course made the presence of a queen (such as Elizabeth I) problematic. There are, of course, always exceptions to this rule. Some cultures are matriarchal, but for the most part the cultures described in Scripture were patriarchal.

While there are still adherents of these traditional patterns, this is no longer an unquestioned assumption. Many have turned to Scripture and asked whether the traditional, patriarchal pattern is divinely inspired or is simply a cultural preference. If the latter is true, then surely we can change the pattern to reflect current views. Perhaps there is even evidence in Scripture that can support such an egalitarian model. It might not be the "majority" opinion, but it is there nonetheless.[26]

Perhaps the place to start in the search for an answer to the question of whether there is a model of equality to be found in Scripture is with the most intimate side of marriage—the sexual relationship. Paul addresses this question 1 Corinthians 7. Finding it necessary to respond to questions about sexual issues in the community, he addresses married couples as if they are equals. Paul's response stands in sharp contrast to the question the Corinthians posed to him. A group within the church asserted the principle that "it is not good for a man not to touch a woman" (1b). Paul answers them by setting up a male-female parallelism in verses 2-4. Then in verse 5, Paul calls on spouses to mutually agree on the subject of sexual abstinence.

In the area of sexual relations between husbands and wives, Paul directed spouses to fulfill their "conjugal rights," or sexual

---

26 Scott Bartchy, "Power, Submission, and Sexual Identity among the Early Christians," in *Essays on New Testament Christianity*, C. Robert Wetzel, ed., (Cincinnati: Standard Publishing Company, 1978), p 57.

needs and desires, to one another (vs. 3). Paul expanded this idea further in verse four to include the question of authority in the sexual relationship, and by implication the marriage relationship itself. Paul began by stating the traditional Greco-Roman and Jewish position, that the husband and not the wife had authority over the wife's body. Paul's male readers would have affirmed this premise, but then he added a non-traditional twist. Not only does the husband have authority of the wife's body, but the wife, and not the husband, had authority over the husband's body (vs. 4). In doing this Paul has overthrown the traditional understandings of authority and provided a new paradigm for understanding the marriage relationship as one of complete mutuality.

As noted above, standing at the center of the question of male/female relationships is the way in which authority is going to be utilized. Women were supposed to submit to the men in their lives. Consider the way in which early Christians women are told to submit to their husbands and follow Sarah's example of calling her husband Abraham, lord (1 Peter 3:1-7). That vision, however, gets challenged in the way in which Paul lays out his argument about sexual behavior in 1 Corinthians 7.

In instructing the Corinthians about who has "authority" over the body of the other, Paul uses the Greek word *exousiazo.* In this context it appears that Paul's definition of the exercise of authority assumes a reciprocal relationship. In his definition of this word in one of the leading dictionaries of biblical words, Woerner Foerster writes:

> Paul is not saying here that each partner has a right to the body of the other, but that each forgoes the right to freely dispose of his own body. He is thus enjoining those who are married not to rule over one another but to mutually serve one another even in the marriage questions.[27]

---

27   Woerner Foerster, "*Exousiazo,*" *Theological Dictionary of the New Testament*, Gerhard Kittle, ed., Geoffrey Bromiley, trans., (Grand Rapids: Wm. B. Eerdmans Publishing Co., 1968), 2:574-575.

For Paul, it would appear, authority involves service and not rule. Perhaps the best way to put this is to envision a relationship of mutual submission.

As we've seen, in 1 Corinthians 7:1-7 Paul speaks of marriage as being a partnership of equals (at least in the context of sexual intimacy). While there is likelihood that Paul didn't write the Ephesian letter, it is possible to read 1 Corinthians 7 in conversation with Ephesians 5:21. In Ephesians 5:21 members of the body of Christ are called upon to submit themselves to each other in reverence for Christ. That is, the principle of mutuality is to define the relationships of Christians. Then the passage moves into the relationship of husbands and wives. Wives are called upon to live out this relationship of mutual submission with their husbands, while husbands are called to love their wives sacrificially. Is this not a call to live in submission to the other?[28] Don Williams has effectively expressed this principle.

> This surprising expression of sexual equality and surrender again presupposes and defends the absolute equality of the sexes at their most intimate encounter. Each is to surrender his or her body to the other partner. Each is lord over the other's body. Paul presupposes that mutual love and self-giving will be expressed in our sexuality. No ego-trips, no will to power, no seduction or rape is tolerated. Here is mutual surrender. Here is the meeting of each other's needs and desires. The last thing in Paul's mind is male dominance or egotism. If sexual relations express the identity of mutual surrender and employment of each other's bodies for sexual fulfillment. As Christ gave himself for us, so we give ourselves to each other.[29]

If, it would seem, we are neither male nor female, but one in Christ then gender distinctions should not define the way in which we relate to each other (Galatians 3:28). Instead, we have the freedom to pursue equality among the sexes.

28 Robert D. Cornwall, *Ephesians: A Participatory Study Guide*, (Gonzales, FL: Energion Publications, 2010), pp. 72-76.
29 Don Williams, *The Apostle Paul and Women in the Church*, (Ventura, CA: Regal Books, 1977), 54.

The principle of reciprocal authority or mutual submission is developed by Paul in verses 2-4 of 1 Corinthians 7, and is followed in verses 5-6 with the development of the principle of joint decision making in marriage. Paul writes: "Do not deprive one another, except perhaps by agreement for a set time, to devote yourselves to prayer, and then come together again, so that Satan may not tempt you because of your lack of self-control." *The New International Version* brings out with even greater clarity the key phrase, which reads: "except by mutual consent." This phrase is important, because this is the only example in the New Testament where decision making in marriage is discussed, and it stresses the importance of mutuality.

In verse 5 of 1 Corinthians 7 Paul addresses those who advocate permanent abstinence from sexual intercourse in marriage on spiritual grounds. Although Paul concedes that spouses might set aside time away from each other for the purpose of prayer, they must do this together and then come back together, lest they be tempted to seek sexual fulfillment outside the marriage. Even then to Paul it is only a concession and not an expectation that one would feel the need to abstain from sex in order to pursue a time of prayer.

Although the focus of Paul's attention in verses 5-6 is the issue of sexual abstinence and infidelity, the key is mutual agreement. In context, there is a contrast between prostitution, which is one-sided (1 Corinthians 6:12-20), Paul calls for the sexual relationship in marriage to be "completely two-sided." This idea of "two-sided marriage" is rooted in the Greek word *symphonia*, which we can translate as "mutual agreement" or as "with one voice." The intent of verse 4 then is to remind sexual partners that they don't have automatic control of their own bodies.[30]

In the case of the sexual relationship the decision to refrain from that relationship should come by way of mutual agreement (*symphonia*). It is important to note here that Paul did not appeal

---

30 Bartchy, "Power, Submission, and Sexual Identity among the Early Christians," p. 59.

to the husband as the "spiritual leader" or "head of the family." Instead, Paul instructs married partners to decide together what is appropriate to their own spiritual welfare. It would seem that this passage, which relates so directly to the shared spiritual life of husband and wife, rules out the idea of the husband being the sole "spiritual leader."

The traditional model for marriage relationships emphasizes hierarchy or chain of command. The implicit message of this model is that women are by nature inferior to men, and therefore need male guidance. Therefore, due to their mental and/or physical inferiority, women should submit to their husbands (or fathers). This perspective colors the way that families structure themselves, but it also influences the way they interpret biblical passages such as Ephesians 5:22-33.[31]

Although many traditionalists deny that they view women as being inferior to men, the way they envision male-female relationships in practice belie that claim. Resisting women in leadership roles, including the ordained ministry, is at least suggestive of such a view. It isn't that there are no differences between men and women—the question is whether these differences imply subordination.

If we affirm the essential equality of the sexes, then male dominance cannot be affirmed. I would suggest that in 1 Corinthians 7:1-7 Paul implies that men and women are not only created as equals but that they should relate to each other on the basis of mutual submission. If this is true, then should we not also read Ephesians 5 in the same light? That is, if 1 Corinthians 7 teaches mutual submission in the context of marriage, then should we not look to this principle in our reading of texts like Ephesians 5? If this is true, then perhaps passages like 1 Corinthians 14, where Paul appears to silence women in church should be seen as a culturally-relative directive that no longer applies as originally understood. That is, Paul is concerned about how the church is seen from outside, and feels the need to rein in those who have celebrated too greatly their freedom in Christ.

31 Cornwall, *Ephesians,* pp. 72-76.

We can find several important implications for understanding of marriage and sexuality embedded in I Corinthians 7. First, Paul goes to great lengths to speak equally to both husband and wife. Second he never equates sexual intercourse solely with procreation; therefore, sexuality can be enjoyed as an end in itself within the context of marriage. A third implication is found in verse 6, where Paul insists that sex does not interfere with one's spirituality. Finally, Paul does not in any way suggest that everyone should be married (though he does believe that if a person has strong sexual desires then in all likelihood that person should marry).

If the issue here is one of equality in the marriage partnership, it doesn't matter if the partners are of the same gender or not. Marriage is a partnership of equals. That said, each couple will need to determine together how this partnership of equals will be lived out in practice. What is true for the sexual relationship is also true of the spiritual life of the couple. Notice that Paul never appeals to the husband as the spiritual leader of the home. Instead, he calls on the two spouses to decide together when and if they will separate for spiritual retreat. This isn't necessarily the easiest or quickest mode of decision-making, but in the end it will be the most satisfying for both partners.

If there is this "minority report" that affirms equality, why do patriarchal ideas remain so ingrained in our society? Is it the Bible or the way we read it that reinforces the patterns with which many were raised (those of us who are Baby-Boomers know this pattern quite well)? Patricia Gundry, whose book *Heirs Together* proved to be a catalyst for change within Evangelical circles when it was published in the 1980s, notes that "mutual submission was a *principle* given to guide relationships between *all* believers. The verses following verse 21 (Ephesians 5) tell how to work it out in three of the most unequal relationships in the society of that day."[32] To tell women to submit, children to obey their parents, and slaves to obey their masters was nothing new, but in each case the author

---

32 Patricia Gundry, *Heirs Together*, (Grand Rapids: Zondervan Books, 1980), p. 95.

of Ephesians modifies the traditional understanding in such a way as to lift the pairs to a position of equality. Therefore, Paul tells husbands to love their wives, "just as Christ loved the church and gave himself up for her" (Ephesians 5:25). If we understand the way in which Christ loves the church, then we can see Paul calling on husbands to take up a position of servanthood to their wives (Mark 10:45). Husbands are not to lord it over their wives (as they would normally do), but instead love them fully, seeking to be a servant. As a result, they would be putting themselves in a position of submitting to their wives.

What then is mutual submission? It is a principle that affirms that each person in a marriage relationship—or in any relationship—is of equal value (1 Corinthians 7:4). Mutual submission requires that a person not demand their full rights but recognize and value the rights of the other (1 Corinthians 7:3). It also means that decisions should be made together and whenever possible should be based on consensus (7:5).

Each couple must work out for themselves how this principle will be implemented. Patricia Gundry comments that "we need to be able to share equally in all the ways we can, in work, responsibility, pleasure, and opportunity."[33] She goes further to define what an egalitarian marriage might look like.

> But when I say equal, I don't mean "same as." I mean equal in opportunity, equal in value, equal in personhood. I mean a relationship in which neither dominates or misuses the other, where decisions are made together when it is reasonable to do so. I mean a relationship of equal persons not a relationship in which the partners must be carbon copies of each other.[34]

Differences don't require subordination. They simply mean that each person will accomplish their activities and roles differently. I'd use the word complement, but unfortunately this word has come to mean something less than equal. Since both male and

---

33 Gundry, *Heirs Together*, p.123.
34 Gundry, *Heirs Together*, p.136.

female are created in the image of God (Genesis 1:27), the differences that exist between male and female are God-given and are designed for the purpose of mutual enjoyment. In a marriage based on the principle of equal partnership, each spouse is encouraged to grow and develop his or her gifts and talents and abilities, not as a means of competition but as a complement to the other. No longer should we encourage women to bury their intellects, gifts, dreams, and talents so that she can attract a husband or not hurt his ego. Each partner should find fulfillment in encouraging the other to develop God-given gifts, and one spouse should not gain fulfillment at the expense of the other.

Mutual submission involves mutual responsibilities. Women cannot expect to be shielded from the need to make decisions or face the world with both its temptations and its opportunities. Unless we accept the verdict that women are inferior to men, then we cannot adopt the position that women need to be protected from life's responsibilities.

The theme of equality, which is established by Paul in Galatians 3:28, continually arises in 1 Corinthians 7:1-7. The question that faces the reader of Paul concerns whether it is possible for him to teach equality at one point and then a strict subordinationism and hierarchy at another point. The conclusion that I draw here is that Paul affirms the principle of mutual submission. He may not have understood all the implications of the principle but contemporary Christians can find sufficient support for the principle of mutual submission in these texts. If men and women are equal in the home, then we must assume that they are equal in the church.

It seems illogical to speak of human equality and then deny people access to certain opportunities simply because of their gender, race, or social class. This is not equality; rather it is sexism, racism, and classism. This type of discrimination should find no place in the church of Jesus Christ where all are one in Christ (Galatians 3:28). This principle does not rule out the need for leadership in the church but it does require that our determination of qualifications should be based on gifts, character, and call, not gender, race, or class. In the end, it would seem that the phrase marriage equality covers a number of realms of existence.

A Call to Reflection and Conversation

1. What is patriarchy? How does it manifest itself in our culture?

2. What is equality and how do you understand it being expressed in human relationships including marriage?

3. How does Paul describe the relationship of married couples in 1 Corinthians 7? Does this differ from or help us better understand Ephesians 5?

4. If you are married or have been married, how are decisions made with regard to the family?

5. How might same-gender and opposite-gender relationships be affected by the way we understand partnerships of equals?

A Call to Action

As individuals or as a group, research cultural patterns that define relationships between persons of the opposite gender and of the same gender, discerning whether these patterns are equal or not. Look to see whether these patterns are changing. For instance, compare Christian, Jewish, Muslim, and Hindu patterns.

A Call to Prayer

> *You have created us, O God, in your own image so that we might share your presence with the world. May we reflect that sense of equality present in your own being in our own relationships, so that all relationships, but especially the covenant partnership of marriage will reflect the equality with which you have equipped us with in creation. Amen.*

CHAPTER 8

FRUITFUL AND MULTIPLYING: CHILDREN AND THE EXPANDING COMMUNITY

Genesis 1:26-31

According to the Psalmist, children are a blessing to the righteous (Psalm 37:26). That very well may be, but having children isn't a necessary element in successful marriage. Nonetheless many marriages, perhaps even a majority, do produce children, even if procreation isn't the final purpose of marriage. After all, with the variety of modern forms of contraception available, couples can decide both when and if they are going to have children. Same-gender couples have choices as well, including adoption, surrogacy, and in vitro fertilization, just to name a few possibilities. In other words, in our modern context "having children" is a decision not an inevitability.

You will find the words "be fruitful and multiply" in Genesis 1, after God creates the first humans on the sixth day. After creating the man and the woman God tells them to be "fruitful and multiply, and fill the earth and subdue it" (Genesis 1:28). That mandate seems to have been largely fulfilled. We have filled most of the earth! Thus, in our context procreation is a matter of personal choice.

Although some religious groups continue to promote large families, family size in much of the developed world, including the United States, has been shrinking for several decades. In my own family situation, I have one brother who does not have any children of his own, while my wife has one brother who has two, as yet, unmarried daughters. We have one child, who has yet to move toward finding a spouse and reproducing another generation—if that should be his choice. Could it be that worries about population growth getting out of control, at least in the "developed world," are premature?

Should a couple decide to have a child or multiple children (by whatever means they deem appropriate), these children often are a blessing to the family. While they can be a challenge, especially when parents find themselves in difficult life situations, most parents feel blessed by the choice they have made. Once the decision to bring a child into the world has been made, parents are charged with helping their children grow up into happy and productive citizens of the world, so they can take up their divinely established role of being stewards of creation (Genesis 1:28-31).

The world into which children are being welcomed today is very different from the one that welcomed me. It is also quite different from the world described in Scripture. Thus, the Bible doesn't provide us with an up-to-date manual for raising children. That doesn't mean, however, that we can't learn something valuable from our readings of Scripture. We simply need to be aware of the differences in contexts.

If we're going to consider the biblical witness concerning the role of children in the life of the family, perhaps one of the best places to start is with the first letter to Timothy. This letter offers a mentor's advice to a young pastor about the life of ministry. The letter's author (traditionally thought to be Paul) gives advice on the selection of congregational leaders. Regarding the selection of bishops or elders, Timothy is told to select a man (it was assumed by the author of the letter that these leaders would be male) who would "manage his own household well, keeping his *children submissive and respectful in every way*" (1 Timothy 3:4). The *Common English Bible* renders this directive in a somewhat softer manner: Bishops should manage their own households well— "they should see that their children are *obedient with complete respect*." Whatever the translation, the emphasis is placed on obedience and respect. That is a rather heavy burden to place on a pastor, is it not? If this is the ideal—the pastor will need to have *obedient* and *respectful* children. If not that person isn't qualified for leadership in the church. If this is the biblical standard, how does it translate to the real world—then and now? Where do we find a divinely authorized model that we can implement?

The ideal and reality rarely see eye to eye, and such is the case here. Scripture offers some rather tragic pictures of parent-child and sibling relationships. Consider the story of the first family. Adam and Eve have two children—the brothers Cain and Abel. Both brothers bring offerings to God, unfortunately for Cain, God prefers Abel's offering. This slight stirs up Cain's anger against his brother, whom he kills. Then, in a conversation that continues to push on us, God asks Cain where his brother is. In response, Cain answers: "Am I my brother's keeper?" Yes, sibling rivalry—and a violent version—appears in the history of the very first biblical family. So, would you consider Adam and Eve good parents?

Moving on, what about Abraham and Sarah? What should we make of their parenting style? Remember how Abraham sent away one wife and her child (Ishmael), letting them fend for themselves because Sarah was jealous. When it came to their child, Abraham was ready to sacrifice Isaac to God—though God called off the challenge just in the nick of time, which saved Isaac's life. Moving on a generation, Isaac has two sons, who we're told starting wrestling for dominance in the womb. When they reached early adulthood, the now elderly Isaac needed to pass on his patrimony (his inheritance) to the eldest son. That would be Esau, who was Isaac's favored son. His wife, Rebekah, wanted her favorite—Jacob—to get the blessing even though he was the youngest, even if by only a nose. Even though her husband wanted to bless Esau, Rebekah helped Jacob deceive Isaac into giving him the blessing instead of Esau. This little event would lead to Jacob's estrangement from his brother and his decision to flee to the house of Laban, his uncle. He did this in part because he needed to obtain a wife, but he also left home because he had to stay clear of his angry brother. If we're still in need of evidence of dysfunctional family life, we only need to look at the story of Jacob's own children, especially Joseph, who was Jacob's favorite. Joseph's arrogance landed him in

Egypt, having been sold into slavery by his angry older brothers. This is only Genesis!

The family stories recorded in the Hebrew Bible continue with more accounts of dysfunctional families. Consider the story of Eli's sons, who are unfit to succeed him as priest. The torch gets passed to Samuel, whom Eli raised, but his children aren't up to the job of leading Israel either. This leads the people to call for a king, so they can be like everyone else. The second king is David, whom Scripture calls a man after God's own heart. He's a great king and warrior, but he doesn't get high marks as either a husband or a father. Consider that one son—Absalom—tries to overthrow his father, while another rapes his half-sister. The latter event leads to a bloody sibling feud (1 and 2 Samuel). If we're going by the standards of leadership laid out in 1 Timothy 3, then David fails to live up to those standards.

On and on it goes. There were good kings whose children failed to live up to the standards of their father. Consider Hezekiah, one of Judah's greatest and holiest kings, who is succeeded by his son Manasseh, who is considered one of the worst. The same could be said of Josiah, who is also considered a holy and great king. He leads Judah into a season of national revival—both politically and religiously. Unfortunately, his own sons were not "chips off the old block" and before too long the nation fell to the Babylonians who destroyed the Temple and carried its elite into exile. Even though Israel had been commanded to honor fathers and mothers, in reality things were a lot more complex during the period covered by our Old Testament.

Moving to the New Testament, the story that stands out to me is found in Luke 2. Jesus and has family have made a pilgrimage to Jerusalem for the Passover. When the time came for the family to return home to Nazareth, Mary and Joseph join up with their caravan and head north. Somewhere along the route the parents discover that their twelve-year-old son was missing. Having made this discovery, they return to Jerusalem. After they search the city they find him hanging out in the Temple talking theology with the priests and other religious teachers. These teachers are amazed at his knowledge, but Mary is more than perturbed that her child chose to wander off. I hear in the story Mary scolding her son, telling him that she and Joseph were worried sick and that he shouldn't try this stunt again. Her reaction is understandable. Most parents get anxious when they can't find their children. Besides, in our day if you leave your child behind in the big city you will likely face charges of child neglect and endangerment. If you watched the movie, you may have enjoyed the antics displayed in the *Home Alone* movies, but in real life that would be no laughing manner. As for Jesus' reply to his mother, might we not read this as typical teenage bravado? He tells his mother: "Why were you searching for me? Did you not know that I must be in my Father's house?" (Luke 2:41-50). The story, of course, ends on a happy note. They return to Nazareth—although the parents don't understand what Jesus was saying to them (parents rarely understand their children). From then on he is an obedient child, increasing "in wisdom and years, and in divine and human favor" (Luke 2:51-52).

What should we make of all of these stories that reveal the dysfunctional nature of these leading families in the biblical story? What do they tell us about the possibility that we should expect to find biblical models of family life in its pages? Could it be that family life and child rearing is not as easy as we would want? That isn't to say that Scripture cannot speak to family life, it's just that the examples might not be as helpful as we would like.

Many years ago I attended a seminar that promised to provide biblical principles for family life. In reality this rather popular seminar was based on proof-texts that were aligned with a rather narrow patriarchal view of family life. What I learned in the long run is that it is foolhardy to expect to find "biblical principles" that would transcend time and place. Having said this, can we not find relevant words in Scripture that might speak to our own day?

Consider the call to honor one's parents, which we find in the Ten Commandments. This sounds right, but what do we make of the rest of the command, which calls on the community to put to death those who curse one's parents (Exodus 21:17). I think that most of us would see this as not "fitting the crime," and we would want to reject it as being over the top (perhaps because none of us would be around if we followed this literally). What should we make of the Proverb that boldly declares that to spare the rod is to spoil the child? The NRSV actually reads this way: "Those who spare the rod hate their children, but those who love them are diligent to discipline them" (Proverbs 13:24). This had been an acceptable disciplinary model for centuries, and it continues to have its advocates to this day, even if it isn't favored by pediatricians, psychologists, law enforcement and judges. Nonetheless you will find many who believe that the decision to spare the rod is the root cause of our societal woes. One can also make the case that beating your child only teaches that child that violence is an acceptable response to others.

One of the things we often forget when we read the biblical story is that children played a different role in ancient societies. Boys were favored over girls, because sons were considered "a heritage from the Lord, the fruit of the womb a reward" (Psalm 127:3). According to the Psalmist, they are "like arrows in the hand of a warrior" (vs. 4). Yes, and "happy is the man who has a quiver full of them" (vs. 5). That verse has given rise to a movement that opposes the use of birth control methods and celebrates exceptionally large families. It was understandable that an agrarian society would value sons, for they were a source of labor. Sons were also expected to provide for their aged parents. If we look closely at ancient family patterns, we will discover that there wasn't the same sentimentality then that often drives modern American visions of the place of children in the family and in society. Today we value children not for what they can produce (though we want them to be productive members of society), but for who they are as individuals, regardless of their productivity.

If most of our biblical examples of family life suggest the presence of dysfunctionality, and the methods of child-rearing present in the text would not be considered acceptable for proper parenting today, what can we learn from the texts?

Considering that many parents find themselves becoming increasingly stressed about the fate of their children, worrying about whether their children are being properly nurtured, perhaps the most important lesson found here is one of grace. It is quite likely that we have come to think that each generation should improve upon their parent's lot in life, which leads to parents becoming frustrated by the flattening out of opportunity. Parents seem to believe they must do everything they can to make sure their children are emotionally, physically, and even spiritually whole. Often this is expressed through the provision of material goods. Those of us who grew up with black and white TVs that broadcast at most three or four channels are often bemused to watch children as young as two or three playing with their tablets and smart phones. At the same time, it seems clear that parents are worrying that they can't offer their own children more than what they received from their parents. Improvement in status seems to have hit a wall, which causes increasing frustration for parents (and perhaps their children as well). Whereas once a college education was something few could expect to achieve, now most American families, at least those in the middle class, assume that college is a necessity. Since a college education no longer brings the rewards it once did, many younger adults are finding themselves going deeper in debt to finance graduate education. One of the results is that marriage is postponed as is starting a family.

Perhaps the biblical story can show parents that the expectation of perfection isn't realistic. Indeed, it's quite possible that children need more structure and guidance than we've been led to believe by the experts. Despite all our good efforts, it's possible that the current generation of children (or their children) will not succeed in the same way as previous generations expected. At the same time, it may turn out that even "poor parenting" doesn't necessarily ruin the lives of society's children. Yes, parents should do their best, but in the end one's parenting isn't the sole determiner of success.

Remember that Joseph started out with a few difficulties, many of his own making, but in the end he did pretty well for himself.

Despite the challenges of parenthood, most families find that their children are a blessing. For his part, despite not being a parent, Jesus valued children. We see this in the scene where the disciples seek to prevent the children who were being brought to be blessed from bothering Jesus. His time was too important to waste on children, which is how his disciples viewed these interlopers. Jesus rebuked the disciples and called the children to him, offering a blessing to each of them. His message to the disciples was this: "Let the little children come to me, and do not stop them; for it is to such as these that the kingdom of heaven belongs" (Matthew 19:14). Perhaps modern parents are overly sentimental about their children. Perhaps they are overly permissive and dote on them. At the same time, we should remember that Jesus saw them as a blessing and as signs of the kingdom.

Children can be a blessing to a marriage, however they come to be part of the family. We should celebrate loving families, for it may be true that the "glory of children is their parents" (Proverbs 17:6).

A Call to Reflection and Conversation

1. What was your childhood like? What was the relationship that you had with your parents?

2. If you have children of your own, how do you understand the role of raising them to maturity? Is this a stressful calling? Why?

3. When you read the biblical stories about family life, what message do you hear? Does this surprise you?

4. What message can you take from the biblical story about modern family life?

5. In what way are children a challenge and/or blessing?

A Call to Action

Take an inventory of your congregation's resources and support network for parents and their children. If you discern a need for more, work together on a plan to enhance the congregation's ability to support parents and love their children.

A CALL TO PRAYER

> *Bless our children with healthful bodies, with good understandings, with the graces and gifts of the Spirit, with sweet dispositions, and holy habits; and sanctify them throughout their bodies, souls and spirits, and keep them unblamable to the coming of our Lord Jesus Christ.* Jeremy Taylor, 1613-1667 (The Complete Book of Christian Prayer.)

CHAPTER 9

MARRIAGE, BROKENNESS, AND THE REALITY OF DIVORCE

Mark 10:2-12

We have discovered that the need for companionship and community is deeply rooted in human nature. It is, one might say, a reflection of being created in the image of God. In the first creation story, a poetic statement of God's creative activity, we hear God say to God's self: "Let *us* create humankind in *our* image," and so "in the image of God he created them; male and female he created them" (Genesis 1:26-27). The use of the plural here invites speculation, and theological speculation isn't the point here—but it does invite us to consider within the oneness that is God there is a plurality of existence—a community within the one. The Christian doctrine of the Trinity is one way of expressing this sense of plurality within the oneness of God.

The Genesis story begins with two stories of God's creation of humanity as male and female. That is, there is differentiation within the species, suggesting that community and companionship are part of the human condition. When we move past Genesis 2 into Genesis 3 the story takes a dark turn. In Genesis 3, brokenness enters the picture. Even as we watch the relationship between God and humanity become damaged, we also see that the relationship between human beings is damaged as well. The truth that is embedded in this story is that all human relationships are to some extent broken and fragmented. This includes the most intimate of human relationships—that of marriage and family. We can even destroy the things meant to bring us joy and happiness. Yes, we are hardhearted people who betray those we love most.

Why is humanity broken? Why do we sabotage our lives and the lives of others? The Bible calls this brokenness sin. Like a virus that eats away at our inner being, sin eats away at us, slowly working its curse of death within us. Every aspect of human life is vulnerable to this malignancy of the human spirit.

It is no secret that many marriages today are in distress. We know about the high divorce rates in our society, even within the church. No sector of the community is unaffected. The reality of this brokenness has led many, especially the children of divorced parents, to avoid getting married rather than experience the eventual dissolution of the bond. While we seem to be feeling the pangs of brokenness with greater intensity today, divorce is nothing new. Perhaps it is more acceptable than before, but that doesn't make any less challenging.

Cheryl and I have been married for more than thirty years, which by some standards is a long time. But whether a couple has been married five years or fifty years, it is unlikely that any couple will have lived together without experiencing a few bumps along the way. I wish I could say that Cheryl and I have never argued or disagreed; that we had never hurt each other or disappointed the other. Unfortunately, I cannot make that claim. On too many occasions sin has crept in and disrupted our lives. Cheryl and I love each other and we are committed to our marriage, but this doesn't mean we are not capable of sabotaging God's gift to us. Of course we aren't alone in this, but it wasn't supposed to be this way. At least that's the message of Scripture.

In Genesis 2 God looks at the man and realizes that it is not good for the man to be alone. Relief comes for the man only after God creates from the man, a "helper fit for him," someone who was "flesh of his flesh and bone of his bone." And God saw that it was good. But then sin crept in and wiped out the harmony. It didn't take long for the honeymoon to end.

This issue of brokenness came before Jesus as he headed toward Jerusalem. Pharisees came and asked his opinion on divorce. Is it allowed, they asked? Now, they already knew the answer to that question, but they wanted to draw him into a debate over the grounds for divorce. The Pharisees were divided into two groups; some took a strict position but others were more lenient. They wanted to know on which side Jesus stood. His answer would alienate at least one party of the Pharisees, but Jesus didn't fall into the trap. Instead of answering their question, he turned the conversation to God's ideal for marriage. He acknowledged that Moses had allowed divorce, but this was because of the hardness of their hearts. So, while divorce was allowed, that was not God's ideal. In the new realm, as Jesus lays it out in Mark 10, there is no room for divorce. If one divorces and remarries, one commits adultery. Matthew does offer an exception. If one party breaks the covenant (unchastity), then the offended party may sue for divorce. Paul also offers an exception—in the case of religiously mixed marriages (1 Corinthians 7:10-11). Apart from these exceptions, the ideal was a life-long covenant relationship.

In turning our attention to God's ideal, Jesus takes us beyond what the law allows. Looking back to Genesis 1 and 2, Jesus says, "from the beginning of creation `God made them male and female'." And, "for this reason a man shall leave his father and mother and be joined to his wife, and the two shall become one flesh." As we have seen, becoming one flesh can mean more than sexual union. In addition to sexual union it can also speak of kinship patterns. With this union of persons and thus of families, something new has come into existence. It is a new creation, which is not merely the merging of two halves of one whole. The idea of a fifty-fifty marriage has been popular over the past few decades, but as Walter Wangerin points out, when we think of ourselves as fractions we discover that "these two halves don't fit perfectly together." Instead of a fifty-fifty relationship, Wangerin suggests that think in terms of three complete beings: the couple and the relationship between them. Both partners serve this relationship, benefit from it, and yet neither of them is exactly like the relationship.

"This relationship is itself very much like a living being--like a baby born from you both. It has its own character. It enters existence infantile, when you speak vows to one another. It comes cuddly and lovely, but very weak and in need of care and nourishment. As time goes on, as this baby-relationship grows up, it becomes stronger and stronger until it serves and protects you in return. This `being', this living thing, this relationship which needs you both (the whole of each of you), but which is *not you* (it is not the two of you added together, because it is distinct from either one of you) -- that is your "oneness."[35]

This relationship is God's gift to us, and this is why Jesus says to us: "What God has joined together, let no one separate." Don't let your brokenness destroy this union. Instead, nourish your relationship, respect it, and invest yourself in it. Marriage brings with it great blessings, but the relationship between the human partners is always a fragile thing because we come into it as two broken people.

Yes, we are hardhearted people. Remember, Genesis 3 follows Genesis 2, and in Genesis 3 sin enters the picture. The relationship crumbles as these two people find themselves divided against each other. They blame each other for their mistakes. The man seeks to rule over the woman, oppressing her. In spite of this, the woman still seeks out a relationship. What was once wonderful becomes broken and unattractive. Therefore, the law allowed a man to divorce his wife. It should be noted here that "Moses" did not allow a woman to divorce her husband (Deuteronomy 24:1-4).

While this might not have been what God intended for humanity, it reflects the reality of human experience. I know about this reality; I am the child of divorce. I have experienced firsthand the effects of what happens when brokenness takes hold of a marriage and therefore a family. I have seen how painful it is for a relationship to die, to see promises violated.

When Cheryl and I were married we promised to receive each other joyfully as partners, "to love and to cherish from this day forward—in times of poverty and times of prosperity, in times of

---

35 Walter Wangerin, *As for Me and My House,* (Nashville: Thomas Nelson Publishers, 1987), 44-46.

sickness and times of God health—to love and to enjoy until death shall separate us." When we made that promise, we didn't leave any room for divorce. We made the promise to live together and love each other until the time of our deaths. Of course, it hasn't always been easy to keep this promise. We have argued and we have fought and there have been times of silence between us. I say this to my own shame, and yet, we have remained true to our promise, "till death shall separate us." Every day we depend on God's grace and God's forgiveness, to help us stay on this path of faithfulness. Every couple that has stayed together for the long haul, has had to work through times of brokenness, whether that be sickness, poverty, disagreement, and perhaps even unfaithfulness. Yes, it is only by God's grace that we can forgive each other.

Wangerin has written a helpful, and revealing account of a period of his own marriage where the relationship with his wife was damaged. As he tells it, it wasn't that he had been unfaithful or had become a bad person; he just neglected his relationship with his wife. In his attempt to be faithful to his duties as a pastor, he had forgotten his wife. As time passed she became angry and bitter, and a wall of separation appeared between them. Not only did they stop talking, but his wife would recoil at his touch. After months of carrying this bitterness within her, his spouse let him know the reason for her pain, but that did not end the silence. They continued to live together, but they did so without love and without forgiveness.

He writes movingly of this time of distress in their marriage:

> I didn't so much as brush her back when I crawled into bed. And once in bed I lay stone still for fear of shaking the mattress and waking her. Did she sleep then? I don't know, though she looked sallow and sick in the daylight. For my own part, my heart hammered all night long. Sometimes she rose in darkness to pace the house; and then I cried because the bed was empty and because I could not help her in her hurt: I didn't have the right even to try. I restrained myself in silence. I played with the kids. I preached, a pure hypocrite, the poet

of the pulpit. And always the tears trembled just behind my eyes, even at church. But I could live without love.[36]

Wangerin tells us that his wife couldn't forgive him because his "sin was greater than her capacity to forgive, had lasted longer than her kindness, had grown more oppressive than her goodness." His sin, he writes, was the "murder of her spirit, the unholy violation of her sole identity—the blithe assumption of her presence, as though she were furniture."[37] Although she could not forgive him, Jesus could and one day that forgiveness did work its way through her and it restored her love for him. I know of what he speaks, for I too have on occasion murdered Cheryl's spirit. I have taken her for granted and I have tested her ability to forgive, but I am thankful for God's forgiveness that has allowed her to forgive me.

There are times, however, when a relationship becomes so distorted that there is really no other option but divorce. When this happens, a death occurs, not the death of the two people, but of the relationship that existed between them. If such an occasion occurs then the loss of something precious must be mourned, and God's grace must be invited into the picture to bring healing.

While the divine intention is that marriage should be for a lifetime, our human reality means that divorce is a possible outcome of a broken relationship. I do not want those who have been divorced to hear my words as words of condemnation. Instead I hope they are heard as an invitation to experience God's healing grace and reconciliation, for in Christ all things become new (2 Corinthians 5:17).

The ideal for marriage—whether one is gay or straight—is for the relationship to grow and mature. For this to occur we must nourish the relationship by giving ourselves completely to the other. If the flame begins to die out, then we should try to rekindle it. If one is contemplating marriage, and seeing it as a daunting calling, it is important to recognize that a couple's journey together is not easy. At the same time, it can be a wonderful journey. Because of the

---

36 Wangerin, *As for Me,* 90.
37 Story told in *passim* in Wangerin, pp. 65-91.

growing numbers of divorces, there is an increasing tendency to go into marriage assuming that it won't last until "death do us part." Quite often that assumption becomes a self-fulfilling prophecy.

Moses, Jesus said, provided the option of divorce as recognition of brokenness. Jesus points us back to the ideal. The question then, for us today, concerns how we experience the reality of broken relationships, especially those relationships that are beyond restoring to their earlier place. For some it is simply necessary to let go of what was and move forward into a new reality. Jesus doesn't speak in this space about this option, but his overall message is one of reconciliation and newness of life. He continually offers a word of healing and hope. The gospel brings grace. And such is the reality that we take hold of here.

While Jesus upholds the ideal, the reality is that not every couple will find it possible to continue the journey together. Lewis Smedes speaks of the "myth of the indestructible marriage," a myth that doesn't fit our human realities today. What we can understand, he suggests, is the sense that "marriage is a covenant between two people, a covenant created by their wills and therefore breakable by their wills. . . When will fails, the marriage dies. It ought not to have died, but it did die."[38] Divorce is a legal remedy that allows two people to make the necessary arrangements so that when their relationship is no longer tenable they can start new lives. Of course, once married, the lives of these two people will always be entangled, especially if there are children involved. When we think of divorce spiritually, it would be better to think in terms of the death of the relationship, which Scripture allows as permission to remarry. With death comes a new opportunity to begin a new life (and in my mind the opportunity for remarriage). As Smedes puts it: "The gospel of grace then opens up new possibilities for a new vow, a new commitment of two selves in the face of an uncertain future, and a new entrée to a life of covenant-keeping."[39]

---

38 Smedes, *Mere Morality,* p. 179.
39 Ibid. p. 181.

A Call to Reflection and Conversation

1. What do you make of the growing numbers of divorces in our society? What are the causes?

2. How do you think the church should respond to divorce?

3. Jesus seems to take a rather negative view of divorce. Why might that be?

4. Why do you think that Matthew offers exceptions that aren't in Mark? Do the exceptions help make better sense of the reality of divorce?

5. In the discussion above, it is argued that spiritually, divorce is the death of a covenant relationship. What is your response to this argument?

6. How does divorce fit with God's intention for life-long covenant relationships?

7. How do we live in grace so that the wounds of broken relationships might be healed?

A Call to Action

As a group do some research on the prevalence of divorce in the broader community. In addition, check out the divorce laws in your state. Are they strict or lenient? Do they require couples to declare a cause or is it more no-fault? What do you make of these laws?

A Call to Prayer

O Lord, we pray for all those who, full of confidence and love,
Once chose a partner for life,
And are now alone after final separation.
May they all receive the gift of time,
So that hurt and bitterness may be redeemed by healing and love,
Personal weakness by your strength,
Inner despair by the joy of knowing you and serving others;
Through Jesus Christ our Lord. Amen. (Chalice Worship, p. 369)

CHAPTER 10

BEYOND MARRIAGE AND FAMILY

Luke 20:27-38

Every culture values family, though family can take many different forms—most of which are culturally defined. In most cultures, some kind of ceremony will be performed that binds persons and families together. Some marriages are arranged by families and others are the choice of the partners. Traditionally marriage has been understood to include at least one male and one female, though there are variations on that theme. In recent years a growing number of people have expanded their understanding of who is covered by the marriage bond to include same-gender couples. In 2015 the voters of Ireland and the Supreme Court in the United States declared marriage equality the law of the land. Some have argued that these changes of definition damage the holy estate of marriage. But, is this really true?

The debate over marriage equality has definitely broadened the conversation and has increased the number of invested persons. What is needed, Gerald Schlabach suggests, is a definition of marriage that is workable for today. Schlabach notes that Augustine offered three "goods of marriage." These are permanence, faithfulness, and fruitfulness. Building on this, as well as Paul's discussion of marriage as the cure for lust, he defines marriage—a definition shared earlier—as "the communally sealed bond of lifelong intimate mutual care between two people that creates humanity's most basic unit of kinship, thus allowing human beings to build sustained networks of society."[40] There is nothing in this definition that limits it to heterosexual marriages. What it does is address the

---

40 Gerald Schlabach, "What is Marriage Now?" pp. 23-24.

problem of contingency; the sense that marriage is irrelevant to the good ordering of society.

In our conversations to this point we have seen that there is no one biblical definition of marriage, and that all understandings of marriage are culturally defined. At the same time Scripture does address the fundamental realities of marriage. It speaks to the good of permanence, faithfulness, and fruitfulness. It also addresses the challenges faced by married couples, including the possibility that human brokenness can lead to dysfunction in marriages and within families. At the same time there is the promise of grace that can heal and restore, even if the marriage itself dies (divorce). At the same time, we have recognized that while we all need companions in life, not all persons will marry. Indeed, Paul suggests that for the good of God's realm it is better to be single (celibate) than to be married. Along the way we have had to deal with the fact that the biblical story emerged in patriarchal societies and that it therefore reflects to some degree that context. At the same time, we have discovered that there has always been a minority report that challenges the patriarchal narrative. Therefore, while there are clear differences between that age and this age, there are important similarities present within the biblical story itself.

Marriage (with its varied frameworks) may play an important role in human society, but marriage does not carry eternal value. That is, there is often a common hope within families that in death they will be reunited with their loved ones—including their spouses. This hope, however, doesn't appear to have scriptural warrant, though some faith traditions, including Mormonism, make this promise. Mormon teachings suggest that marriages performed in a Mormon Temple are consecrated not only for the present life, but also for the next life. Again this isn't the biblical view. Nonetheless, many within mainstream Christianity believe that family life will continue into the next life in much the same way it does in this life.

It might be helpful as we near the end of this series of conversations about marriage to hear from Jesus. Consider, for instance, the occasion upon which he rebuffed the attempts by his own family to have an audience with him. They were, it appears, trying to take him home because he had become an embarrassment to the family. He responded to them by claiming that his true family was not his blood relations but those who do the will of his Father in heaven (Matthew 12:46-50). Surely this a much broader definition of family than is often taught in the church, even if we talk of church being family.

Jesus takes this question further in a conversation with a group of Sadducees (Luke 20:27-38). While the central issue here is the resurrection and not marriage, the way in which the question is posed and answered does reflect on the eternal value of marriage and family. The Sadducees, who didn't believe in the resurrection, sought to embarrass Jesus with a question about levirate marriage. They hoped they could show how ridiculous resurrection thinking was by asking him to declare who a woman in such a marriage would be married to in the resurrection, since she had been married to several brothers without producing a child.

It is important to remember that ancient Judaism lacked a developed sense of the afterlife. Therefore, one's legacy was to be found in one's progeny (children). Think of the promise made to Abraham and Sarah that through their descendants, by way of Isaac, the nations would be blessed. Many families, even today, are concerned about passing on the family name. It's one of the reasons why many families prize having a son. In American culture it has been the tradition that the wife would take on the husband's name, so that their children would continue carrying on the patrilineal line from one generation to another. Therefore, should my son fail to marry and have a son, a branch of the Cornwall family will have reached its end.

With levirate marriage, if a man died, leaving a widow, but had no child (hopefully a male child) at the time of his death, then a kinsman, usually a younger brother, was to marry the widow. This kinsman hopefully would father a child in the name of this now deceased brother, so that the family line could continue.

One of the best examples of this practice is found in the story of Tamar in the Genesis story. In this story Judah, the son of Jacob and Leah, married a Canaanite woman named Shua. In time this couple had several sons, the oldest being Er. Judah obtained for Er a wife named Tamar. Unfortunately, he dies—more specifically God kills him because of his wickedness—leaving Tamar without a husband and a child to carry on the family name. Wanting to make sure that the family line continued, Judah sent his second son, Onan, to marry Tamar. But he too was wicked. As Genesis puts it, "since Onan knew that the offspring would not be his, he spilled his semen on the ground whenever he went into his brother's wife, so that he would not give offspring to his brother."[41] This displeased God, and he dies. Since the third son was too young to be given in marriage to Tamar, Judah tells her to wait till he's grown up. She followed his directions for a while, but when she realized that Judah wasn't going to follow through on his promise of offering her the third brother (perhaps Judah had begun to see a pattern developing) she decided to take things into her own hands. After Judah's wife Shua died, Tamar hatched a plan to trap Judah into providing her with the necessary child. She would do this by playing the prostitute and entrapping Judah. In the course of time, Tamar became pregnant with twins. When her father-in-law confronted her about her apparent adultery, she was able to prove that Judah was the father of Perez and Zerah (Genesis 38). Having been outed by Tamar, Judah accepted the children as his own. This story once again illustrates the differing expectations of men and women when it came to sexuality. It was the woman, not the man, who was held accountable. A man could, as Judah did, engage in extra-marital behavior without much penalty. A woman, on the other hand, was considered property and had to remain chaste, except in the context of marriage.

---

41 It is good to remember that the story of Onan has nothing to do with masturbation. The judgment about spilling his seed here has to do with his unwillingness to fulfill a cultural obligation.

With this background we can hear the question posed by the Sadducees to Jesus. They offer a hypothetical situation. Suppose there are seven brothers, none of whom are successful in their attempt to provide a child—they failed to leave a legacy. So, they ask Jesus if he's right and there is a resurrection, and this woman has had seven husbands, none of whom did she provide with a child, then who would she belong to in the afterlife? Note here that the question has to do with ownership of the woman.

The Sadducees want to see what kind of a biblical interpreter Jesus is. Is he a good traditionalist like them or is he a liberal like the Pharisees? To them, the idea of levirate marriage served as a good example of why the idea of the resurrection is really a silly notion. In their reading of Scripture, there is no resurrection, so the right answer would be that none of them would be her husband since none of them would experience an afterlife. Instead of answering the way they expected, Jesus simply turns the tables on them by suggesting that marriage is really not that important in the long scheme of things. Jesus resolves the dilemma by proclaiming that their example of levirate marriage is irrelevant, since in the new realm there is no need for marriage. That's because there will be no need for procreation. Of course, this may mean that there won't be any heavenly family reunions either.

Why is that? Well, marriage, family, and procreation have a lot to do with security. Even the Genesis 2 story, which I believe focuses on the need for companionship, is about security. In the new realm of God, however, security is to be found in God and not one's mate or one's progeny. Remember that for Jesus, one's brothers and sisters, and even mother (remember that for Jesus and his context, God is one's Father), is to be found in the community of faith. Perhaps one reason why the Sadducees, as members of a wealthy sector of society, did not find the idea of resurrection to be compelling is that they found sufficient security in this life, and therefore needed no promise of more to come in the next life. They took to heart the promise that wealth was a sign of blessing, and as persons of wealth they had sufficient blessings.

While marriage isn't the focus of the passage, it does raise an important set of questions relating to the ultimate value of marriage and family. If marriage and family are transient values, then should the church emphasize "family ministry" and "family values" in a way that excludes or isolates those who are not married? Does it change the focus of our ministries? The issue is not whether we should nurture strong marriages or strong families, but is this the foundation of the ministry of the church? It also raises questions about the way in which we envision roles in church and society for both men and women.

Due to the division of roles and the limitations placed on women in ancient societies, marriage and family was the key to survival. Levirate marriage not only provided a legacy, it provided security to a woman who had been completely dependent for her survival on her husband. Without any social safety net, she was extremely vulnerable unless there was family—either a husband or a child. This may be one reason why Laban made sure that Jacob married Leah before he offered Rachel to Jacob in marriage. If Rachel was married first, that would have placed a mark against Leah's marriageability. In the case of the levirate system, a widow became the wife (and thus the property) of the one who claimed her. Consider the story of Ruth and Naomi. In marrying Boaz, her nearest kinsman willing to claim her as his wife, Ruth provided a future for herself and for Naomi. In producing a child, Naomi's line continued through Boaz.

The woman in the Gospel story, however, ends up being married seven times but never has a child. Considering that barrenness was considered a curse, then this woman's failure to bear a son meant that she was a burden to the six younger brothers who likewise were considered failures in their duty to the eldest brother. While the Sadducees had no need for resurrection, perhaps the promise of resurrection would have been for the woman in the story a sign of justice and freedom. Not only would she no longer be a burden to another, but she would no longer be the property of another.

As one who has been married for more than three decades, I would say that by-and-large marriage is something that is good and valuable. In many ways the modern understanding of marriage as a partnership of equals is a significant improvement on what was present in the first century and before. Women are no longer—in Western society—the property of the husband (or her father). A woman can choose her destiny—whether she wants to be married, whether she wants to work, whether she wants to have children. This not only frees women from earlier burdens, it frees men as well. They have choices. They can, if they have children, choose to stay home and care for the children, while the spouse (male or female) works outside the home. But marriage is not the ultimate. It's not the only way in which humans can find fulfillment. And as Jesus reminds us—there is no marriage in heaven. Whatever the after-life looks like, our current patterns of family life, including marriage, will not continue to exist.

Marriage and family are social goods, but for Jesus they do not carry either eternal or ultimate value. The purpose of the church is not to focus on upholding family values, if by family we mean the nuclear family. After all, for Jesus, the church is our ultimate family, for the church is where we live in relationship with our elder brother—Jesus the Christ. If family is a social good, then perhaps the church can find new and creative ways of providing family for those who are in need of the benefits that families provide, but in which many lack access.

A Call to Reflection and Conversation

1. What is family? What role does it play in your life? In the broader society?

2. In what way is the church a family? Is the same as with the biological family?

3. How do you envision ongoing relationships with family after death?

4. What do you make of Jesus' statements about there being no marriage in heaven?

5. Jesus seems to broaden the definition of family in a way that diminishes traditional biological bonds and extends them to those who share his religious identity. What is the message here for us?

6. Having explored questions of marriage and family, what is family? Does faith have anything substantive to say on the subject?

A CALL TO ACTION

Consider together ways in which the church can be family to those who do not have traditional family settings. How, for instance, might older members of the church serve as surrogate grandparents to children whose own grandparents might be deceased or live far away? Make a plan of action that will help the church be truly family to each other.

A CALL TO PRAYER

Father of all mankind, make the roof of my house wide enough for all opinions, oil the door of my house so it opens easily to friend and stranger and set such a table in my house that my whole family may speak kindly and freely around it.
Source Unknown (Hawaii)

BIBLIOGRAPHY

Achtemeier, Mark. *The Bible's Yes to Same-Sex Marriage: An Evangelical's Change of Heart*. Louisville: Westminster John Knox Press, 2014.

Augustine. *Confessions (Penguin Classics)*. Translated by R.S. Pine-Coffin. New York: Penguin Books, 1961.

Bartchy, S. Scott. "Power, Submission, and Sexual Identity among the Early Christians," in *Essays on New Testament Christianity*. Edited by C. Robert Wetzel. Cincinnati: Standard Publishing Company, 1978.

Cartwright, Colbert S. and O.I. Cricket Harrison. *Chalice Worship*. St. Louis: Chalice Press, 1997.

The Complete Book of Christian Prayer. New York: Continuum Publishing Co., 1995.

Cornwall, Robert D. *Ephesians: A Participatory Study Guide*. Gonzalez, FL: Energion Publications, 2010.

_____. *Unfettered Spirit: Spiritual Gifts for a New Great Awakening*. Gonzalez, FL: Energion Publications, 2013.

Cox, Harvey and Stephanie Paulsell. *Lamentations and the Song of Songs (Belief: A Theological Commentary)*. Louisville: Westminster John Knox Press, 2012.

Farley, Margaret. *A Framework for Christian Social Ethics*. New York: Continuum Books, 2006.

Foerster, Woerner. "*Exousiazo.*" *Theological Dictionary of the New Testament*. Edited by Gerhard Kittle. Translated by Geoffrey Bromiley. Grand Rapids: Wm. B. Eerdmans Publishing Co., 1968, 2:574-575.

Gundry, Patricia. *Heirs Together.* Grand Rapids: Zondervan Books, 1980.

Gushee, David. *Changing Our Mind.* Second edition. Canton, MI: Read the Spirit Books, 2015.

Johnson, William Stacy. *A Time to Embrace: Same-Sex Relationships in Religion, Law, and Politics,* 2nd edition. Grand Rapids: Wm. B. Eerdmans Publishing Co., 2012.

Jones, Tony. *There Are Two Marriages: A Manifesto on Marriage.* Minneapolis: Jopa Productions, 2011.

LaRochelle, Robert. *A Home United,* Gonzalez, FL: Energion Publications, 2015.

Lester, Andrew D. and Judith L. *It Takes Two: The Joy of Intimate Marriage.* Louisville: Westminster John Knox Press, 1998.

Long, Kimberly Bracken and David Maxwell, Editors. *Inclusive Marriage Services: A Wedding Sourcebook.* Louisville: Westminster John Knox Press, 2015.

McClendon, James William. *Systematic Theology: Ethics.* Nashville: Abingdon Press, 1986.

Mattox, Nathan. "'A Wild Ass at Home in the Wilderness': Fidelity and the Life of Faith in a Hypersexualized, Consumer-driven Culture." In *Oh God, Oh God, Oh God! Young Adults Speak Out about Sexuality & Christian Spirituality.* Edited by Heather Godsey and Lara Blackwood Pickrel. St. Louis: Chalice Press, 2010.

Oord, Thomas Jay. *The Nature of Love. A Theology.* St. Louis: Chalice Press, 2010.

Piatt, Christian. *Post Christian: What's Left, Can We Fix It, Do We Care?* New York: Jericho Books, 2014.

Schlabach, Gerald. "What Is Marriage Now? A Pauline Case for Same-Sex Marriage." *The Christian Century,* (October 29, 2014), Vol. 31, No. 22, pp. 24.

Smedes, Lewis B. *Mere Morality: What God Expects from Ordinary People.* Grand Rapids: Wm. B. Eerdmans Publishing Company, 1983.

Wangerin, Walter. *As for Me and My House.* Nashville: Thomas Nelson Publishers, 1987.

Williams, Don. *The Apostle Paul and Women in the Church,* Ventura, CA: Regal Books, 1977.

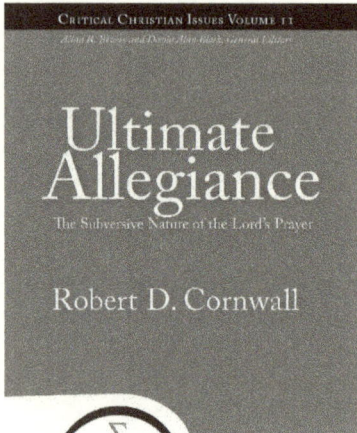

CRITICAL CHRISTIAN ISSUES VOLUME 11

Ultimate Allegiance

The Subversive Nature of the Lord's Prayer

Robert D. Cornwall

AREOPAGUS
CRITICAL CHRISTIAN ISSUES

It's a beautiful thing to watch a pastor teaching her or his people with wisdom and grace. In Bob Cornwall's hands the old bones of the Lord's Prayer take breath and life.

Jason Byassee
Research Fellow in Theology & Leadership
Duke Divinity School

Bob Cornwall here shows that the gifts of the Spirit are not owned by the pentecostal-charismatic wing of the church. Rather, the time is now for mainline churches to reappropriate the full spectrum of the spiritual gifts for their contemporary tasks. The result may include the sought for revitalization of the historic Protestant tradition as it seeks to bear appropriate witness to the living Christ in a pluralistic world.

Amos Young
Dean, Divinity School, Regent University
Author of *Spirit of Love*

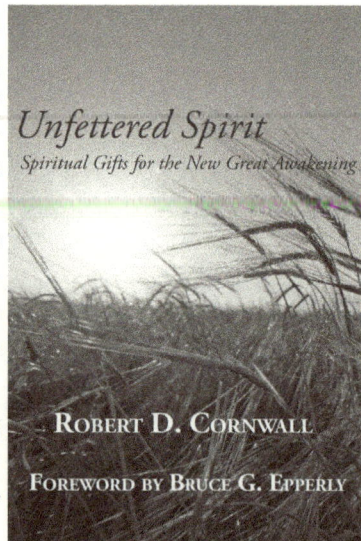

Unfettered Spirit
Spiritual Gifts for the New Great Awakening

ROBERT D. CORNWALL

FOREWORD BY BRUCE G. EPPERLY

MORE FROM ENERGION PUBLICATIONS

Personal Study

The Jesus Manifesto	David Moffett-Moore	$9.99
When People Speak for God	Henry Neufeld	$17.99
The Sacred Journey	Chris Surber	$11.99

Christian Living

It's All Greek to Me	David Alan Black	$3.99
Grief: Finding the Candle of Light	Jody Neufeld	$8.99
My Life Story	Becky Lynn Black	$14.99
Crossing the Street	Robert LaRochelle	$16.99
Life as Pilgrimage	David Moffett-Moore	14.99

Bible Study

From Inspiration to Understanding	Edward W. H. Vick	$24.99
Meditations on the Letters of Paul	Herold Weiss	$14.99
Philippians: A Participatory Study Guide	Bruce Epperly	$9.99
Ephesians: A Participatory Study Guide	Robert D. Cornwall	$9.99
Ecclesiastes: A Participatory Study Guide	Russell Meek	$9.99
Colossians and Philemon: A Participatory Study Guide	Allan R. Bevere	12.99

Theology

Creation in Scripture	Herold Weiss	$12.99
Creation: the Christian Doctrine	Edward W. H. Vick	$12.99
The Politics of Witness	Allan R. Bevere	$9.99
Ultimate Allegiance	Robert D. Cornwall	$9.99
History and Christian Faith	Edward W. H. Vick	$9.99
The Journey to the Undiscovered Country	William Powell Tuck	$9.99
Process Theology	Bruce G. Epperly	$4.99

Ministry

Clergy Table Talk	Kent Ira Groff	$9.99
In Changing Times	Ron Higdon	$14.99

Generous Quantity Discounts Available
Dealer Inquiries Welcome
Energion Publications — P.O. Box 841
Gonzalez, FL 32560
Website: http://energionpubs.com
Phone: (850) 525-3916